AMERICAN LEGAL ETHICS

*A RETROSPECTIVE
FROM 1997 TO 2018*

FRANCIS G.X. PILEGGI, ESQ.

outskirts
press

Table of Contents

About the American Inns of Court
and
The Bencher

The following articles, by Francis G.X. Pileggi, Esq., are a compilation of legal ethics columns originally published in *The Bencher*, a bi-monthly magazine of the American Inns of Court. The American Inns of Court is an association of lawyers, judges, and other legal professionals from all levels and backgrounds who share a passion for professional excellence. Through regular meetings, members are able to build and strengthen professional relationships; discuss fundamental concerns about professionalism and pressing legal issues of the day; share experiences and advice; exhort the utmost passion and dedication for the law; provide mentoring opportunities; and advance the highest levels of integrity, ethics, and civility. Our Inns have gained a national and international reputation as an organization that bridges the gap between formal law school education and legal practice by offering career-long continuing education in the Common Law tradition.

This uniquely non-partisan association encourages meaningful mentoring relationships. We are one of the very few legal organizations that involve the whole spectrum of the profession: from law students to supreme court justices; every level of federal and state judges, small firms to large firms; legal educators to law students.

In this collegial environment, outside the courtroom and pressure of daily practice, members discuss legal practice, principles, and methods. Academicians, specialized practitioners, and complementing generalists provide a mix of skill, theory, experience, and passion. This fluid, side-by-side approach allows seasoned judges and attorneys to help shape students and newer lawyers with practical guidance in serving the law and seeking justice.

The Bencher is the flagship publication of the American Inns of Court. Circulated to all members, it is published six times a year. The purpose of *The Bencher* is to provide a regular communication link among the national office, Inns, and members of the American Inns of Court. Each issue features articles written to a central theme such as legal ethics, professionalism, civility, or mentoring. Current circulation is more than 31,000 by mail or electronic PDF.

Celebrating 20 Years of Ethics Columns in *The Bencher*
Pileggi, Ratnaswamy Still Going Strong after Two Decades
By Jennifer J. Salopek

While attending an American Inns of Court event in Washington, DC, Francis Pileggi heard an announcement that *The Bencher* was looking for a new ethics columnist. He volunteered, and his first column was published in the January/February 1997 issue. John Ratnaswamy also stepped up, so it was suggested that the two men alternate the responsibilities, each authoring three columns per year. Two decades later, they are still going strong. "I did not anticipate that I would be doing this for 20 years!" Pileggi says.

Pileggi, now a partner at the law firm of Eckert Seamans in Wilmington, Delaware, had an active interest in legal ethics and in writing. An early adopter of social media, he created and maintains the Delaware Corporate and Commercial Litigation Blog, and has published widely. His approach to ethics and to the column has evolved over time, he says. "I was much more focused then on the theoretical aspects and pure principles of legal ethics. Now I tend to focus more on the applications in every practice."

Ratnaswamy is a founding partner of Rooney Rippie & Ratnaswamy in Chicago, Illinois. At the time he volunteered for the column, in early 1997, his law firm had just added an in-house ethics attorney. "I was interested in legal ethics and wanted more writing opportunities," he says. Ratnaswamy serves as an adjunct professor of legal ethics at the Northwestern University School of Law.

A look through selected columns from the Pileggi/Ratnaswamy era is a bit like a time capsule of the evolution of legal ethics in the United States. Together, the two have covered such diverse topics as professionalism in a high-tech legal world, prosecutorial discretion, conflicts of interest, attorney–client privilege, activities leading to bar association sanctions, and many more.

Francis G.X. Pileggi, right, also serves on the Neumann University Board of Trustees and is pictured above at a recent graduation ceremony with Monsignor Fred A. Britto, also a trustee of Neumann University.

When asked where they get their topic ideas, their responses differ. "Originally, I focused on a combination of topics that interested me, and current developments," says Ratnaswamy. "Later, I also started to try covering things people might not know, and occasionally tried to find topics that tied in with the theme of *The Bencher* issue."

Ratnaswamy also draws inspiration from his role as adjunct professor, writing columns in reaction to issues or comments from course participants. An experiential learning course, it features mock activities in which students participate. "There are a lot of ethics rules that aren't intuitive. I try not to give an opinion, but to set things up to lead to the correct thinking."

It's difficult to teach ethics in the abstract, he notes. "The Socratic method makes it harder to recognize things when they're on your doorstep. Practice and visualization make it easier to do the right thing."

Only once, Ratnaswamy says, did he use a personal experience as inspiration for a column. In November/December 1997, he published a column entitled, "Inadvertent Disclosure of Confidential Information in Discovery." He wrote:

In 1991, I experienced one of those moments when a lawyer suddenly confronts an exigent question of professional responsibility. While reviewing documents produced by my opposing counsel in discovery, I realized that he had provided me with "unredacted" originals of documents that had been "redacted" in order to protect his client's privileged communications. After reflection on the relevant considerations, I advised my opposing counsel of his error....

Given the unsettled and varying state of the law, a lawyer who receives inadvertently produced confidential information should carefully consider the salient ethical and evidentiary law in the relevant jurisdiction(s), as well as the underlying moral and ethical principles.

As for Pileggi, he gets his topic ideas primarily from his firm's in-house general counsel, other lawyers, his brother, who is a judge, and, less frequently, recent decisions. "Very few of my columns include court opinions," he says. "Most arise out of my research and are occasioned by bar association actions or public reprimands." In March/April 2011, however, he addressed the Rhode Island Supreme

Court ruling that law firms must be allowed to withdraw from representing clients who don't pay their bills, calling it "an opinion that should be welcomed by all lawyers who prefer not to be forced to work for free." Rarely are Pileggi's topics controversial, but he expects his most recent column to be more so, as he tackles the new American Bar Association amendment regarding verbal discrimination. "Many people think it's too amorphous, and I think there will be increased litigation over what it means," he says.

The columns highlight how much the world has changed in 20 years. For example, in Pileggi's first column, he discussed the responsibility of lawyers to respect methods of communication and allow ample time for opponents and courts to respond. In discussing whether to send legal communications via email, he noted that "email is not yet universal, and… it may very soon be as ubiquitous as the fax machine." At the time, he felt that it was inappropriate to email legal communications, because "most email… is not immediately brought to the attention of the addressee as in the case of correspondence placed on a person's desk." In this era when everyone is glued to their mobile phones 24/7, it's difficult to remember a time when a hard-copy letter would get more attention.

In May/June 2005, Pileggi returned to technology as a topic, noting that "legal ethics now requires some knowledge of software." He explained the concept of metadata that can be hidden in a word processing document and that, through revisions and various versions, could reveal client confidences.

In a column for July/August 2015, Pileggi took a totally different approach, explaining and commenting on professionalism through the example of a judge newly inducted to the U.S. District Court for the Eastern District of Pennsylvania. He wrote:

Articles about professionalism more often than not emphasize how lawyers should behave. Professionalism also must be expected of the judiciary, and it remains equally important for judges to treat lawyers and others who appear before them with the same respect, courtesy, and dignity that all lawyers should exhibit, both orally and in writing.

Looking back over their tenure as columnists, Pileggi and Ratnaswamy reflected on the continuing need for the column and how professionalism and civility in the legal profession have evolved.

"In the 1960s, people had a high opinion of lawyers. They saw them as heroes, and it attracted a lot of students to law school," says Ratnaswamy.

Ratnaswamy, pictured left, an avid Chicago Cubs fan, recently experienced his team winning the 2016 World Series.

"In the 1980s, lawyers decided that the way to get ahead was to be a jerk. I do think that has decreased, though. I don't hear people complaining as much as they used to."

Pileggi's observations are driven by his practice area in the commercial haven of Delaware, which has seen not only an increase of lawyers over the past 30 years, but an influx of law firms headquartered elsewhere, opening offices in Delaware. "The more lawyers you get, behaviors and norms of conduct change," he says. "However, things are still collegial and genteel. There is a sense of pride that is a trademark of the Delaware bar."

Both men say they've gained from their experience as columnists—but not in terms of clients. Pileggi notes that he got a new client as a result of a column, but only one. The reward actually comes, he says, from the learning that ensues from his research. "I enjoy writing the column and am happy I have done it. I have gained much better insight into the issues—it's been a learning experience." Ratnaswamy expresses a similar sentiment, saying, "I have sometimes been surprised as I have researched a rule or an issue, and I have learned by doing." ◆

—Jennifer J. Salopek is a freelance writer in McLean, Virginia. She can be reached at jjsalopek@outlook.com.

Our legal system, with all of its many virtues, is not designed, and perhaps cannot be designed, to function effectively when those who participate in it do not comply with the Rules of Professional Conduct and basic notions of fairness. Even the best enforcement by disciplinary counsel does not often restore offended parties to their emotional and financial condition prior to being subjected to the offending behavior of an errant practitioner. Nonetheless, I recognize that although the answers to some ethical issues are clear cut, some factual situations provide no easy answer. That is, the facts of some cases present a clear "black and white" decision while others present different hues of gray. One story and two cases illustrate my point.

A priest was hearing confessions one Sunday when a young boy confessed to throwing peanuts into the river. The amused clergyman quickly forgave the boy and sent him on his way. The next penitent was also a young boy who likewise sought forgiveness for throwing peanuts into the river. Again, the priest forgave the boy and dismissed him. When the next person to enter the confessional also appeared to be a young boy, the priest asked, "Did you also throw peanuts into the river?" The boy said, "No, Father, my name is Peanuts." Although this humorous story emphasizes the importance of full disclosure, two reported decisions provide examples of situations that involve issues that do not lend themselves to such easy analysis.

In *Dworkin v. General Motors Corp.*, 906 F.Supp. 273 (E.D.Pa. 1995), the Court addressed the issue of disqualification of a law firm that had filed multiple suits against GM. That firm hired an associate who had previously handled many cases on behalf of GM. The associate's new law firm had often been opposing counsel when the new associate had been representing GM.

The issue of disqualification in such a situation is increasingly common due to the proliferation of attorneys changing law firms several times during their careers. In the *Dworkin* case, the Court ruled, based on the facts presented to it, that the imputed disqualification of the new law firm was not warranted merely due to the prior representation of GM by the new associate, in light of screening procedures implemented a few days prior to the date that the new associate joined the firm. 906 F.Supp. at 283. The Court found

that the controlling Rule of Professional Conduct that governed the outcome of the case was Rule 1.10(b). The version of Rule 1.10(b) adopted by Pennsylvania which the Court interpreted, provides as follows:

> When a lawyer becomes associated with a firm, the firm may not knowingly represent a person in the same or a substantially related matter in which that lawyer, or a firm with which the lawyer was associated, has previously represented a client whose interests are materially adverse to that person and about whom the lawyer had acquired information protected by Rules 1.6 and 1.9(b) that is material to the matter unless:
>
> (1) the disqualified lawyer is screened from any participation in the matter and is apportioned no part of the fee therefrom; and
>
> (2) written notice is promptly given to the appropriate client to enable it to ascertain compliance with the provisions of this rule.

The Court found that Rule 1.9 regarding the prohibition against representing someone in a case against a former client, did not apply because the new associate was neither representing any party against his former client, nor was any evidence presented that the new associate used information relating to his representation of GM to its disadvantage. *Id.* at 278. The Court's reasoning in *Dworkin* relied primarily on the characteristics of the "ethics screen" or "Chinese wall" that barred the new associate from any involvement in the representation of clients by his new firm against the new associate's former client, GM. Noting that the Rules of Professional Conduct did not provide specific guidance as to what constitutes an effective screen, the Court relied on the following factors:

(1) The substantiality of the relationship between the attorney and the former client;

(2) the time lapse between the matters in dispute;

(3) the size of the firm and the number of disqualified attorneys;

(4) the nature of the disqualified attorney's involvement; and

(5) the timing of the wall. *Id.* at 279.

In addition, the Court considered the importance of the following four features of the "ethics screen" or "Chinese wall":

(1) The prohibition of discussion of sensitive materials;

(2) restricted circulation of sensitive documents;

(3) restricted access to files; and

(4) a strong firm policy against breach, including sanctions, physical and/or geographic separation. *Id.* at 280.

The *Dworkin* case involved a firm of four lawyers and the Court found it important to note that the screen also involved such requirements as color coding, or otherwise prominently marking GM files so that they would be readily identifiable from a distance, as well as an office policy that prevented the new associate from entering offices or conference rooms without first establishing that no prohibitive material was either being discussed or was present.

Another reported decision that provides an example of a situation where the dilemma may not be simple, is *McGuinness v. Barnes*, 683 A.2d 862 (N.J.Super. 1994). In the *McGuinness* case, there was no Rule of Professional Conduct at issue, rather the issue was whether an attorney's statement made during a legal seminar that he presented could be used against him in a legal malpractice case. The question presented itself in a motion prior to the legal malpractice trial. In the legal malpractice suit, the plaintiff claimed that the defendant attorney failed to obtain certain hospital records and failed to obtain an expert witness. During the legal seminar that the defendant attorney was presenting, he stated that attorneys handling medical malpractice cases should always obtain hospital records and should find expert witnesses willing to testify on behalf of their clients. The defendant attorney attempted to keep these statements out of his legal malpractice trial based on a First Amendment free speech rationale. The Superior Court of New Jersey was not persuaded by the argument, in which the attorney also sought to create a new privilege based on the First Amendment. Despite the possible negative impact it may have on those who present seminars, the Court found no legal basis for such a new privilege and allowed the statements at the seminar to be used against the attorney for purposes of impeachment and cross-examination. I suppose that this case would only present a problem for someone who might not always practice what they preach.

I invite suggestions for topics of future articles, especially relating to issues that may be unsettled, or recent decisions that shed light on well-established ethical guidelines. You can reach me by phone at (302) 655-3667.

The author is a partner at the Wilmington, Delaware, office of Pileggi, Pileggi and Pileggi. He is licensed to practice in Delaware, Pennsylvania and New Jersey, and is a frequent author and lecturer on topics that include issues of professionalism and ethics.

Free Legal Advice on the Internet, but at What Cost?

Francis G.X. Pileggi, Esquire

Legal issues relating to the Internet are developing as quickly as the Internet itself. Of particular concern are offers of legal advice on the Internet. As the number and content of legal directories grow, so do the number of sites advertising and offering, sometimes free legal advice.

A relatively broad Internet search including search terms such as "legal advice, consultation and consult" yields literally hundreds of thousands of results. Internet sites identified include attorney ads, law firm homepages, legal information sites, and publisher sites offering legal directories, as well as information and access to attorneys and legal corporations. The content of each site varies widely and at least one of each offers some form of purely electronic consultation.

One site, found at "www.freeadvice.com," invites users to submit legal questions via email. The legal questions may be answered for free by attorneys who pay to be on a list of attorneys who receive the inquiries. The site states that it is not a lawyer referral service. However, users are asked to submit their telephone numbers in the event the answering attorney wishes to contact them. Information about attorneys available to answer questions on a particular subject in a geographic area is listed.

The Freeadvice site's "Getting Listed on Free Advice" page represents that an advantage of the service is that "[a]ll the legal information on Free Advice links to our Lawyer Directory." Information on the page also indicates that the service may help to generate business from outside of the state in which the subscribing attorney practices.

Internet sites offering legal advice present serious ethical and professional issues. First, an attorney or law firm may engage in activity on the Internet that may be in violation of the ethical rules of the state or states in which he practices or other states in which his website is viewed or used.

The U.S. Supreme Court, interpreting an Ohio disciplinary rule limiting in-person solicitation, found that the Ohio rule at issue did not prohibit a lawyer, based on the facts of that case, from communicating information to a person about his legal rights, or from recommending that he obtain counsel. *Ohralik v. Ohio State Bar Association*, 436 U.S. 447, 458 (1978). The Court did, however, find that the rule properly prohibited the lawyer from using the information as a bait with which to obtain an agreement to represent the person for a fee. Lawyers may, however, provide legal services without charge provided pecuniary gain is not a substantial motivating factor. Situations will likely arise soon, in which courts will address whether offers of free legal advice, forms or certain information through an on-line legal directory or webpage constitute an "offer" of free legal advice for which pecuniary gain is a substantial motivating factor.

Individual state courts have just begun to examine jurisdictional issues relating to the Internet. A Massachusetts court recently found it had jurisdiction over a party by virtue of an Internet site that solicited business nationwide. See *Hasbro Inc. v. Clue Computing Inc.* 97-10065.

It was not until 1977, that the Supreme Court recognized advertising by attorneys as commercial speech protected by the First and Fourteenth Amendments. See *Bates v. State Bar of Arizona*, 433 U.S. 350 (1977). The Court in *Bates* held that a state may adopt reasonable regulations to ensure that lawyer advertising is not false or misleading, but may not flatly prohibit all lawyer advertising.

Recently, Pennsylvania found that an attorney's webpage is a directory advertisement. In turn, Pennsylvania subjects its attorneys' webpages to the applicable advertising directory rules. See Pennsylvania Ethics Opinion 96-17 (1996). Therefore, if Pennsylvania extends jurisdiction to attorneys whose webpages are used or usable in Pennsylvania it may choose to apply its professional rules regarding webpages to those lawyers in other states. The question ultimately is whether posting information on the World Wide Web constitutes an advertisement, the practice of law, or something otherwise in violation of the law of a particular state.

The question of advertising is vexing. Lawyers occasionally appear on radio, television and in print offering advice of some kind. The most common form of which we are all aware is the call-in radio show. The advice offered on radio call-in shows is typically in a format in which the advice is provided more for "goodwill," as opposed to being a "quid pro quo" for pecuniary gain. Given the substantial expenditure of time and resources required to provide advice on the Internet, such activity may well be viewed as substantially motivated by pecuniary gain.

Efforts such as those being made by Delaware Supreme Court Chief Justice E. Norman Veasey as head of a national study authorized by the National Conference of Chief Justices entitled "A National Study and Action Plan Regarding Lawyer Conduct and Professionalism," perhaps will address Internet issues. Chief Justice Veasey also chairs The Ethics 2000 Commission of the American Bar Association. The Commission will review the Rules of Professional Conduct in an effort to update them in light of current realities.

Tennessee is currently the only state that expressly regulates direct contact by a lawyer with prospective clients on the Internet. Slanina, *Ethically Speaking: Ethics in the Ether*, IN RE:, November 1997, at 14.

As lawyers know, legal problems often present complex issues that may lead to unanticipated results in areas that, to the lay person, appear unrelated. Failure to temper legal advice offered on the Internet may expose users to more substantial legal problems than they had initially.

Most, if not all, sites utilize some form of disclaimer. Disclaimers range from a simple refusal to accept any responsibility for anything, to elaborate recitations including Sale of Goods Warranty disclaimers plucked from U.C.C. Article 2. Perhaps the most common are claims that no attorney client relationship is formed. Assuming no relationship is formed, a user may be left with no recourse if harm results to the user.

In the absence of an attorney client relationship, users have no guarantee that their transmissions will remain confidential. It is not likely that the lay person using such a service knows the implications of relating private information to an attorney where no privileged relationship is formed. Such information may be used against the individual, and in some cases the attorney may actually be required to disclose the information.

Even if a privileged relationship is formed, the information transmitted may not be secure. Email transmission provides little assurance of security. Transmissions are readily susceptible to misdelivery or interception.

Simply determining whether a particular site is legitimate may in itself not be possible. Internet sites offering legal advice are largely unrestricted. Despite rules prohibiting the unauthorized practice of law, in many circumstances, it may be difficult if not impossible to determine the actual source of the information..

Legal advice sites on the Internet may provide a service to members of the public, but the disservice to the public may be substantially greater. Users should be wary of the many pitfalls that may result from acting on or simply obtaining free legal advice. It may be helpful to remember that when you get something for free, you often get what you pay for. ■

Francis G.X. Pileggi is the Managing Partner of the Wilmington, Delaware office of Manta and Welge. He is a frequent writer on issues involving ethics and professionalism.

Contingency Fees Must Be Reasonable

Francis G.X. Pileggi, Esquire

An appellate court in Colorado recently applied Rule of Professional Conduct 1.5 to uphold a jury verdict requiring an attorney to return the full amount of his contingency fee based on the failure of the attorney to prove that the fee was reasonable for the services that he performed. The attorney's client had sued for a refund in the case of *Eich v. Maceau*, Col. Ct. App., No. 96CA1354, Ney, J. (Nov. 28, 1997) (unpublished).

This article summarizes that decision. It does not address whether contingency fees are valid per se. Nor does this article address contingency fee cases such as shareholder derivative suits, where any fee must be approved by the court. *See generally* ABA Formal Opinion 94-389 (December 1994).

Public awareness of contingency fees in general has increased in light of the contested fees now being reviewed by the courts in the various class actions against the major tobacco companies, such as the 15% fee that Texas lawyers are seeking for their part in a $15.3 billion settlement, and 25% that Florida lawyers are seeking out of an $11.3 billion settlement they obtained for the state.

In the *Eich* case, the Colorado Court of Appeals held that it was appropriate for the attorney to be forced to return his entire contingency fee, based on the following facts: The original client of the attorney who was forced to return his contingency fee, was a woman about 72 years of age at the time of the accident. She was a passenger in a vehicle that was hit by a drunk driver. She was hospitalized for five weeks and at the time of the settlement, her medical bills were approximately $70,000. Her injuries included a fractured skull. Approximately three months after taking the case, but prior to filing suit, the attorney obtained the full $100,000 policy limits of the injured woman's uninsured motorist coverage. The attorney also filed suit against the tavern where the drunk driver was served prior to the accident, and also monitored the criminal case against the driver without charging extra. It is not clear, however, what the results were of that additional work, if any.

Approximately a year and a half after the settlement for $100,000, for which the attorney took a one-third fee, the injured party sued for a full refund of the contingency fees collected.

At trial, the attorney's reconstructed time records, which apparently were not created contemporaneously, indicated a total of 44.5 hours on the case at the time the $100,000 policy limits were offered. If calculated based on an hourly rate, the fee received by the attorney would amount to approximately $750 per hour for the work that he performed, which consisted of phone calls and letters. Because the jury found that the attorney's services were without merit or without value, there was no compensation granted under the theory of quantum meruit.

In sum, the appellate court upheld the jury's determination that the attorney failed to prove that the fee charged was reasonable. *Eich v. Maceau*, Col. Ct. App., No. 96CA1354, slip op. at 6, Ney, J. (Nov. 28, 1997) (unpublished). The issue was not raised on appeal whether it was more appropriate for the court, as opposed to the jury, to determine the reasonableness of a fee. The court found that the burden was on the attorney to prove that his fees were reasonable based on Rule of Professional Conduct 1.5, and the appellate court upheld the jury's determination that the value of the attorney's services was zero, thus providing a valid basis for the conclusion that the fees should be returned. *See generally Kovach v. Brownsville Hospital*, 3d Cir., No. 97-3061 (Dec. 23, 1997) (unpublished), *ABA/BNA Lawyers' Manual on Professional Conduct*, (Jan. 17, 1998) at 421 (upholding trial court's reduction of contingency fee agreement from 40% to 25% based on court's supervisory power over members of the bar, unlike non-lawyers who are parties to an agreement); *Hoffert v. General Motors Corp.*, 656 F.2d 161 (5th Cir. 1981) (court may still question contingency fee even if issue is not raised by the parties); *In re Hanna*, 362 S.E.2d 632 (S.C. 1987) (lawyer may not collect any fee for collecting personal injury protection [PIP] benefits disbursed without objection). *Cf. King v. Armstrong*, 518 N.W.2d 336 (Iowa 1994) (award of 50% of recovery not unreasonable in light of facts, such as unlikelihood of recovery). *See also* S. Koniak, *Principled Opinions: Response to Brickman*, 65 Ford. L. Rev. 337 (October 1996) (discussion of ABA Opinion 94-389 which reaffirmed validity of contingency fees).

Unfortunately the standard of reasonableness does not always lend itself to mathematical precision in the context of contingency fees. ∎

Francis G.X. Pileggi is the managing partner of the Wilmington, DE, office of Manta and Welge. He is licensed to practice in Delaware, Pennsylvania and New Jersey, and is a frequent author and lecturer on topics that include issues of professionalism and ethics.

Ethics Rule 1.9 and its Practical Implications

Francis G.X. Pileggi, Esquire

A recurring problem in today's litigious world involves attorney conflicts of interest. This is especially so in the business world which is filled with directors, shareholders and entities, all of which often need complex legal representation. The idea that lawyers owe duties to former clients seems simple enough. It is an outgrowth of the agency law principle that an agent's duties to his principal continue, albeit in reduced scope, after the agency relationship has been terminated. See *Webb v. Du Pont*, 811 F. Supp. 158, 163 (D. Del. 1992).

Lawyers, generally speaking, have no recognized duty to accept a particular client or matter, though once one does accept, a certain amount of freedom is lost to take on new matters, even when the first representation is final. This simple assertion, however, results in numerous law suits and ethical questions every year, especially in the corporate context. Each state's conflict of interest rules give both present and former clients a limited veto power over their lawyer's choice of work.

In a recent Ethics Opinion[1], *Opinion 1997-4 (October 3, 1997)*, the Delaware State Bar Association Committee on Professional Ethics specifically addressed this topic in an interesting factual situation. The issue involved a former director's dismissal from employment by his company for "cause." The director contended that the law firm representing the company had a conflict of interest because of a past client relationship he had with the same firm. The past client relationship took place when the director and nine other directors all engaged the firm's representation to determine the effect of a merger on their employment status. While the law firm did formerly represent the director in the past matter, no one from the firm ever met or directly spoke with the aforementioned director because he was not one of the designated representatives for the director group. However, each of the ten directors paid the firm for its representation and the firm regarded all as clients. The law firm proceeded to represent the company in connection with several other matters and ultimately represented the company in the termination proceedings against the director. The former director strenuously objected to the firm representing the company in his termination action based on their past representation of him in the previous matter. The Delaware Bar Association Ethics Committee looked directly to state rules of professional conduct and Delaware case law to analyze the issue.[2]

Disqualification of an attorney for a conflict is addressed by Rule 1.9[3] which states as follows:

A lawyer who has formerly represented a client in a matter shall not thereafter:

(a) represent another person in the same or a substantially related matter in which that person's interests are materially adverse to the interests of the former client unless the former client consents after consultation[4]; or

(b) use information relating to the representation to the disadvantage of the former client except as Rule 1.6 or Rule 3.3[5] would permit or require with respect to a client or when the information has become generally known. *(amended, effective June 1, 1988)*

The general rule in Delaware courts, as explained in *Nemours Foundation v. Gilbane*, 632 F. Supp. 418, 422 (D. Del. 1986), provides a four-prong "facts and circumstances" test to disqualify counsel. The test requires that:

First, the lawyer must have had an attorney-client relationship with the former client. Second, the present client's matter must either be the same as the matter the lawyer worked on for the first client, or a "substantially related" matter. Third, the interests of the second client must be materially adverse to the interests of the former client. Fourth, the former client must not have consented to the representation after consultation.

Before demonstrating that the interests of the two clients are "materially adverse," it must first be shown that the past and present work is "substantially related."

To establish the "substantially related" element of the test, guidance is provided in *Satellite Financial Planning v. 1st National Bank of Wilmington*, 652 F. Supp. 1281, 1283 (D. Del. 1987). *Satellite* provides that a court must always answer three questions to decide whether the "substantial relationship test" has been met. First, the court must decide what was the nature and scope of the prior representation. Second, what the nature and scope of the present suit against the former client entails. Last, the court must determine whether in the course of the past representation, the client may have disclosed to his attorney any confidences which could be relevant to the present suit. The inquiry must be made with particular attention paid to whether such confidences could be detrimental to the former client in the current situation.

The Delaware Bar Association Ethics Committee found, based on the facts before it, that the third Satellite factor was not met. The Committee used a pragmatic approach and found that while some degree of overlap between past and present matters might have been possible, those elements would be "essentially academic in nature and lacking in practical significance." The Committee, therefore, found that the former director could not meet the burden of establishing that a "substantial relationship" existed between the present and former representations.[6] *Satellite*, 652 F. Supp. at 1283.

This situation, where a client has only *de minimis* communication with his counsel, is more and more likely to occur. It is in this context that the primary purpose of Rule 1.9—to eliminate the opportunity for an attorney who has "switched sides" to use information obtained from the former client in the second proceeding—requires careful scrutiny. See *Richardson v. Hamilton International Corp.*, 469 F.2d 1382, 1385-86 (3rd Cir. 1972) (noting that plaintiff attorney who had previously represented defendant corporation must be disqualified in new matter due to possibility of past acquired information being used in pending action).

I invite suggestions for topics on future articles, especially relating to issues that may be unsettled, or recent decisions that shed light on well-established ethical guidelines. ■

Francis G.X. Pileggi is the managing partner at the Wilmington, DE, office of Manta and Welge. He is licensed to practice in Delaware, Pennsylvania and New Jersey, and is a frequent lecturer on topics that include issues of professionalism and ethics.

1. *The Bar Committee's opinion does not have the force of law. The Disciplinary Counsel of the Delaware Supreme Court is vested with the power to prosecute ethical violations.*

2. *Delaware Supreme Court Chief Justice E. Norman Veasey is currently heading an ABA ethics commission to update the Professional Conduct Rules for the year 2000.*

3. *Delaware Lawyers Rules of Professional Conduct. D.L.R.P.C. 1.6, 1.7 and 1.8 also address conflict of interest issues. See generally, In Re Arlen Mekler, Del. Supr., 689 A.2d 1171 (1996).*

4. *Waiver will not be specifically addressed in this article, however, it is interesting to note that although clients may waive disqualification of their counsel in subsequent litigation, waiver is not effective unless past counsel discloses his intended role on behalf of the new client.*

5. *Rule 1.6 is concerned with the confidentiality of information. It mandates that a lawyer may not, under usual circumstances, reveal information relating to representation of a client. Rule 3.3 is primarily concerned with candor towards the tribunal and states that its rule is applicable even where it is in conflict with Rule 1.6.*

6. *For a recent example of a law firm which was disqualified from representing a party due to past conflicts of interest in relation to Rule 1.9, see Rhoads & Sons, Inc. v. Wooters, 1996 WL 41162 (Del. Ch. 1996).*

An Analysis of Conflicts
Francis G.X. Pileggi, Esquire

An attorney representing both a closely held corporation and a majority shareholder in a buyout by the majority shareholder of minority-held shares faces a potential conflict of interest. In the role as attorney for the corporation, the attorney must protect the best interests of the corporation, and the corporation most likely will want the shares valued at the highest possible price. The majority shareholder, however, may want to pay as little as possible for the minority shares. *See generally, Alayo I Carreras v. Cable West Corporation*, 624 F. Supp. 1167 (D. Puerto Rico 1986) (ordering that an attorney with an economic and proprietary interest in a parent corporation cannot represent the subsidiary as plaintiff against the parent and also be the legal representative of the shareholders).[1]

Although this issue has not produced many reported decisions, an analogous issue has arisen in derivative actions. In a derivative action, the plaintiffs usually are shareholders who bring suit on behalf of the corporation against directors and/or officers for breaches of their fiduciary duties. The corporate directors and/or officers are the main defendants and the corporation is generally considered a "nominal" defendant because the suit has not been brought directly against it. *See Musheno v. Gensemer*, 897 F. Supp. 833 (M.D. Pa. 1995). However, a derivative action places the corporation in the unusual position of a defendant-party with an economic interest in

seeing the plaintiffs prevail if the plaintiffs' claims are legitimate. Courts have confronted the question of whether, in a derivative action, an attorney can serve as both the representative of the defendant-corporation and the representative of the alleged wrongdoers, the defendant-directors/officers.

Courts addressing this question have split between approving such representation or requiring that one of the defendant parties retain separate counsel. *Musheno v. Gensemer, supra.* Most of the earlier court decisions ruled in favor of allowing dual representation. The better view requires that the corporation retain separate counsel. *See Cannon v. U.S. Acoustics Corporation*, 398 F. Supp. 209, 217 (N.D. Ill. 1975), *reversed on other grounds* 532 F.2d 1118 (7th Cir. 1976).

Many of the older derivative action cases justified permitting dual representation by focusing upon the corporation's right of choice in selecting its counsel and the absence of allegations of a conflict or breach of trust by the co-defendant directors. *E.g. Otis & Company v. Pennsylvania R. Co.*, 57 F. Supp. 690 (E.D. Pa. 1944), *aff'd* 155 F.2d 522 (3rd Cir. 1946). Some newer cases reach this same result, although with an apparently more complex understanding of the modern corporate environment. See *Musheno v. Gensemer, supra.* (ordering the appointment of separate counsel for the corporation even though the action did not result in litigation).

Concerns over a corporation's right of choice may become less relevant in a closely-held corporation. The owners and directors remaining after the buyout are often the same parties, and thus in effect, the parties who make choices for the corporation's welfare. However, allegations by minority shareholders of a breach of fiduciary duties by the directors, mandate additional investigation by the attorney, especially where there is more than one shareholder remaining. Over time, courts examining the interests in derivative actions began finding conflicts, especially when there had been allegations of illegal conduct or fraud on the part of the directors or officers. *See generally*, Harry G. Henn and John R. Alexander, *Laws of Corporations*, (1983) (prohibiting common counsel is an appropriate position).

In a widely cited case, *Cannon v. U.S. Acoustics Corporation, supra*, the court disqualified a law firm from representing a corporation and its directors. Because the director-defendants had been accused of misappropriation of corporate funds, the court found that on its face, the complaint raised a potential conflict.

As a result, the *Cannon* court stated that this conflict would present a hardship on the court if a conflict arose in the middle of litigation and necessitated the appointment of new counsel. Specifically addressing the historical approach in derivative action cases of finding a lack of conflict, the court noted that the corporation requires separate counsel, even if "the corporation's right of counsel of their choice is infringed[,] and in a closely held corporation, as here, the financial

---

1. *This article will not address the possible conflict in opposing a minority shareholder, when that party was part of a group of shareholders for whom an attorney initially formed the corporation. Nor does this article directly address prior representation of opposing parties. See generally MRPC 1.13 (stating that a lawyer retained by a corporation "represents the organization acting through its constituents" and may also "represent any of its directors, officers, employees, members, shareholders or other constituents").*

burden is increased.... On balance, the corporation must obtain independent counsel." *Id.* at 220.

While not entirely analogous to the buyout situation, *Cannon* and the modern derivative action decisions present a strong argument for separate counsel in a buyout in certain situations. For example, if there is one majority shareholder and if the incentive underlying a majority shareholder's buyout is the minority shareholder's complaints of serious mismanagement or potentially fraudulent conduct, separate counsel may best protect the interests of both the corporation and the separate shareholders.

The case of *Bell Atlantic Corporation v. Bolger*, 2 F.3d 1304 (3rd Cir. 1993), may provide some guidance. This case addressed the joint representation of a corporation and individual defendants who had reached a settlement agreement with the plaintiffs. The plaintiffs had alleged mismanagement and a breach of the fiduciary duty of care.

The court first noted that under ethical standards, the lawyer's obligation is to the corporation. However, the court added that:

[t]he proposition that the organization is the lawyer's client does not alone resolve the issue. Most derivative actions are a normal incident of an organization's affairs, to be defended by the organization's lawyer like any other suit. However, if the claim involved serious charges of wrongdoing by those in control of the organization, a conflict may arise between the lawyer's duty to the organization and the lawyer's relationship with the board.

Id. at 1316, *citing* ABA Model Rules of Professional Conduct. This finding bolsters arguments for requiring dual representation in a buyout by a majority shareholder of a minority shareholder's interests.

The *Bolger* court referred to Model Rule of Professional Conduct 1.13 to suggest that if a claim involves charges of serious wrongdoing by the parties who control the corporation, a conflict may arise. The court noted that "[w]e have no hesitation in holding that—except in patently frivolous cases—allegations of directors' fraud, intentional misconduct, or self-dealing require separate counsel". *Id. See Rowen v. LeMars Mutual Insurance Company of Iowa*, 230 N.W. 2d 905 (Iowa 1975) (asserting that a court can base disqualification upon a potential conflict of interest rather than a demonstrated one and requiring separate counsel as a preventative method of protecting the law firm from finding itself representing of a corporation and individual defendants who had reached a settlement agreement with the plaintiffs). *See also Scott v. New Drug Services, Inc.*, Del. Ch., 1990 WL 135932 (recognizing that when a derivative action arises under a claim of fraud, as opposed to negligence, the corporation has a more active role which may necessitate the appointment of separate counsel).

Model Rule of Professional Conduct 1.13 (1998 ed.) provides in relevant part as follows:

(a) a lawyer employed or retained by an organization represents the organization acting through its duly authorized constituents.

. . .

(e) a lawyer representing an organization may also represent any of its directors, officers, employees, members, shareholder or other constituents, subject to the provisions of Rule 1.7. If the organization's consent to the dual representation is required by Rule 1.7, the consent shall be given by an appropriate official of the organization other than the individual who is to be represented, or by the shareholders.

The commentary to Rule 1.13 provides in paragraph 11:

The question can arise whether counsel for the organization may defend... [a lawsuit compelling the directors to perform their legal obligations and the supervision of the organization.] Most derivative actions are a normal incident of an organization's affairs, to be defended by the organization's lawyer like any other suit. However, if the claim involves serious charges of wrongdoing by those in control of the organization, a conflict may arise between a lawyer's duty to the organization and the lawyer's relationship with the board. In those circumstances, Rule 1.7 governs who should represent the directors and the organization.

The main problem an attorney will confront in the buyout situation is that the corporation, per se, should not consent to a dual representation without the conflict issue first being addressed. If the directors are also the remaining shareholders (after the buyout), the attorney might be essentially making a request that the directors consent for both the corporation and themselves.

Additional guidance for an attorney confronting these conflict interests come from EC5-15 of the ABA Code of Professional Responsibility (predecessor to the Model Rules of Professional Conduct) which provides:

If a lawyer is requested to undertake or to continue representation of multiple clients having potentially differing interest, he must weigh carefully the possibility that his judgment may be impaired or his loyalty divided if he accepts or continues the employment. He should resolve all doubts against the propriety of the representation.

Further, EC 5-14 stated that:

Maintaining the independence of professional judgment required of a lawyer precludes his acceptance or continuation of employment that will adversely affect his judgment on behalf of or dilute his loyalty to a client. This problem arises whenever a lawyer is asked to represent two or more clients who may have differing interests, whether such interests be conflicting, inconsistent, diverse, or otherwise discordant.

These commentaries support the view that an attorney should remain highly attuned to the conflicts which may arise during dual representation. Factual considerations would include the number of majority shareholders and any allegations by the minority shareholders. Vigilance in addressing issues which arise will ensure than an attorney avoids conflicts in his representative duties. ■

Francis G. X. Pileggi is the managing partner at the Wilmington, DE office of Manta & Welge. He is licensed to practice in Delaware, Pennsylvania and New Jersey, and is a frequent lecturer on topics that include issues of professionalism and ethics.

Ethics Rules and the Internet
Francis G.X. Pileggi, Esquire

The World Wide Web is fast becoming a vital resource for lawyers as a marketing tool. As use of the internet grows at a stunning pace, the number of ethical issues its use poses grows proportionately. The internet enables lawyers with the click of a button to reach a global network without geographical or jurisdictional boundaries. Internet "real time" chats facilitate solicitation. Today the ethical issues related to the internet are in a sorting-out period. Adding to the confusion is the fact that some states have adopted the ABA Model Rules of Professional Conduct, others have adopted modified versions of the ABA Model Rules, while others are still under the Model Code of Professional Responsibility. These differing rules result in different and conflicting standards of regulation.

As the various State Professional Ethics Committees consider the myriad of issues raised by lawyers marketing on the internet, a consensus may be developing. First, the Rules of Professional Conduct that are applicable to lawyers' advertising also apply to websites or "home pages." *See, e.g.,* Pennsylvania Bar Association Ethics Opinion 96-17 (1996); South Carolina Ethics Opinion 94-27 (1995). This, too, is consistent with the U.S. Supreme Court decision in *Zauderer v. Office of Disciplinary Counsel,* 471 U.S. 626, 105 S.Ct. 2265 (1985), wherein the court found that written communication of solicitation aimed at making a profit or drumming-up new business is "advertising." This includes instances where the advertisement provides free legal information to the public and if the site also contains any information about hiring the law firm. Therefore, websites containing information such as lawyer biographies, practice descriptions, contact information, etc. appear to fit the *Zauderer* definition of advertising.

As advertising, any false, fraudulent, deceptive, or misleading communication is prohibited. *See, e.g.,* Model Rule of Professional Conduct 7.1. State regulators intend to ensure

> *"As use of the internet grows at a stunning pace, the number of ethical issues its use poses grows proportionately."*

that internet advertising be monitored to prevent the same sorts of abuses that have been seen in lawyer advertising via other media. Additionally, because websites will be considered advertising, most states will require that a hard copy be preserved for at least one year from any ad posted on the internet whether it is in the form of a home page, bulletin board posting, usenets, etc. *See, e.g.,* Virginia Ethics Opinion A-0110 (1998). In other states, lawyers will be required to submit their website ads for review prior to posting on the internet. *See, e.g.,* Florida and Texas Rules. Further, if the website provides links to any outside sites, lawyers should indicate that such sites are not maintained by that lawyer or lawyer's law firm. *See,* Association of the Bar of the City of New York Committee on Professional and Judicial Ethics, Formal Opinion 1998-2. Disclaimer and

disclosure requirements also must be heeded. *See* Iowa Ethics Opinion 95-21 (1996).

There is less consensus as states grapple with their oversight powers regarding improper advertising or solicitation or the unauthorized practice of law. Especially troubling to the regulatory committees is the "real time" internet conversations that may take place within a particular state's boundaries. *See generally Wall Street Journal,* August 2, 1999 at page B1, "More People Consult the firm of Cyber, Web & Dot-com" (discussing websites that provide free legal advice, such as Nolo.com and Free Advice.com). The Philadelphia Bar Association Committee on Legal Ethics recently suggested in its Opinion 98-6 (March 1998) that prudence suggests that lawyers include in any communication a notice regarding the states in which such lawyers are licensed along with a statement that it is not the lawyers' intent to give advice. Model Rule 8.5(b)(2)(ii) provides a choice of law when lawyers are licensed in more than one state. The rules of the jurisdiction "in which the lawyer principally practices" apply unless the particular conduct clearly has its "predominant effect" in another jurisdiction in which the lawyer is licensed. For attorneys licensed in more than one state, websites should comply with ethics rules on advertising in all states in which they are licensed because there is no way to predict where a website will have a "predominant effect." A lawyer, too, may be subject to discipline by a licensing state if that state decides to invoke its prohibition against misleading advertising, finding that a lawyer's home page is misleading if it suggests that such lawyer can practice in other jurisdictions. Therefore, lawyers should clearly identify where they are licensed to practice.

Lawyers must be mindful, too, that discussion areas enabling communications with individuals may be construed as the beginning of an attorney/client relationship with all attendant duties that such implies, including creation of potential conflicts of interest, expectations of confidentiality and exposure to malpractice. Here, disclaimers may be insufficient to shield a law firm or lawyer from a claim that an attorney/client relationship was in fact established by reason of specific on-line communications.

"Real time" conversations may constitute solicitation thereby additionally subjecting a lawyer to rules regarding solicitation. "In person" communications in personal injury and wrongful death cases may be restricted or prohibited. *See Florida Bar v. Went For It, Inc.*, 515 U.S. 618, 115 S.Ct. 2371, 132 L.Ed.2d 541 (1995), which upheld a Florida disciplinary rule creating a 30-day blackout period after an accident during which victims or relatives could not be solicited. Rule 7.3(b)(1) addresses this, stating:

A lawyer shall not contact, or send a written communication to, a prospective client for the purpose of obtaining professional employment if:

1. the lawyer knows or reasonably should know that the physical, emotional or mental state of the person is such that the person could not exercise reasonable judgment in employing a lawyer.

Because of anonymity afforded by the internet, an attorney should also be concerned with Model Rule 4.2 which states:

In representing a client, a lawyer shall not communicate about the subject of the representation with the party the lawyer knows to be represented by another lawyer in the matter, unless the lawyer has the consent of the other lawyer or is authorized by law to do so.

It is impossible for a lawyer communicating in "real time" through his website to know whether the person with whom he or she is communicating is represented by an attorney. Even if that person is unrepresented, the lawyer cannot tell if the person has interests adverse to existing clients.

In conclusion, a lawyer can probably best minimize his exposure by following the "lowest common denominator" approach of complying with the most restrictive rules of a state wherein he is licensed. Additionally, the lawyer should freely use disclaimers and disclosures throughout his website. Extra caution should be taken with respect to any "real time" communications. ■

Francis G.X. Pileggi is the Managing Partner at the Wilmington, DE office of Manta & Welge. He is licensed to practice in Delaware, Pennsylvania and New Jersey, and is a frequent lecturer on topics that includes issues of professionalism and ethics. Mr. Pileggi is also a national member of the American Inns of Court. The substantial assistance of the firm's summer law clerk, Sherry Bove, in the research and preparation of this article is gratefully acknowledged

Ethics in the Trenches
Francis G.X. Pileggi, Esquire

Most of my ethics articles for the past few years have tended to focus on philosophical ruminations. This one will focus on the more mundane quotidian "hand-to-hand" verbal combat of practicing law, often found in depositions. Obnoxious conduct in depositions is usually not unethical, but that same behavior can be unprofessional. So, what does one do about it, when most judges do not want to be bothered with "traffic cop" disputes, and most clients are not excited about paying you for your efforts to police other lawyers.

Fortunately, there is one case that dealt with deposition conduct that was so egregious, that it was used by a Delaware judge to create a bright line boundary for actions of *deponents* that will subject the deponent's lawyer to a penalty, if that lawyer either acquiesces or does not control the client. In *State v Mumford*, 731 A.2d 831 (Del. Super. 1999), an eminent domain case, the Delaware Superior Court revoked the *pro hac vice* admission of an attorney who both failed to curb his client's abusive deposition conduct and also was arguably encouraging it. Excerpts of the deposition should not be quoted in a genteel publication like this one, but the deponent frequently referred to the questioning attorney in graphic anal terms and most of his phrases included a crude adjective associated with coition. The published opinion in *Mumford* contains sufficient excerpts to give an understanding of why the court reached its conclusion.

The attorney in *Mumford* also violated Delaware Superior Court Civil Rule 30(d)(1) by making longwinded objections that either suggested the

answer to the deponent or were intended to affect the substance of the deponent's testimony (which was tantamount to the rule's prohibition of conferring with the client about his testimony during the deposition or during a break in the deposition). He did this by making the deponent aware of his attorney's concern's about the nature and focus of the pending question, by way of the attorney's speaking objection. In my experience, this is one of the most often abused rules in depositions (although I know that not every state has a rule as clear as Delaware's on this point).

The attorney in *Mumford* also violated the same rule by instructing his client not to answer a question even though it was not necessary to preserve a privilege. *Id.* at 834.

Delaware courts have previously explained the type of behavior that will not be tolerated in depositions in Delaware, but in the most famous opinion on that issue, the malefactor at the deposition was not a Delaware lawyer and for some reason was not admitted *pro hac vice. See Paramount Communications v. QVC*, 637 A.2d 34, 55 n.34 (Del. 1994)(condemning abusive and obstructive language by a defending attorney towards a deposing attorney.) In *Paramount*, the Delaware Supreme Court observed that depositions are the factual battlegrounds that see most of the action in litigation and: "Counsel should never forget that ... as long as the deposition is conducted

under the authority of the rules of this court, counsel are operating as officers of this court." *Id.*

The *Mumford* court relied on the reasoning in *Paramount* and the Delaware State Bar Association's Statement of Principles of Lawyer Conduct, to which the *pro hac vice* admitee is expected to adhere, to emphasize that an attorney does not only represent the client at the deposition, but counsel also has a duty to the court to "ensure the integrity of the discovery process". *Mumford* at 835. We know that in Delaware that includes a duty to control a client who is abusive to the deposing attorney. The defending attorney's failure to restrain his client's repeated profanities , hostility and "soapbox antics", made him deficient in his duty to maintain the integrity of the discovery process. *Id.*

Thus, even when defending a deposition, the defending attorney (at least in Delaware) cannot be passive even if there is no pending question, and must assume a role perhaps similar to the director of a movie by maintaining a minimum level of decorum, at least to the extent of controlling the actions of the client but at the same time not interfering with the questions himself. ∎

Francis G.X. Pileggi is the Managing Partner at the Wilmington, DE office of Manta & Welge. He is licensed to practice in Delaware, Pennsylvania and New Jersey, and is a frequent lecturer on topics that includes issues of professionalism and ethics. Mr. Pileggi is also a national member of the American Inns of Court.

Practicing Law as E-commerce: Is it Ethical?

Francis G.X. Pileggi, Esquire

How will the wave of e-commerce that is affecting almost everyone who works for a living, and how they work for a living, impact the ethical constraints within which lawyers make their living? How will doing business online be treated by the individual state authorities that regulate attorney conduct, for purposes of determining whether an attorney can use the Internet to practice law in any manner similar to the method by which a vendor of other services might use the Internet to engage in e-commerce?

At least one state seems to have addressed the issue based on a guarded presentation of facts. The Board of Commissioners on Grievances and Discipline for the Supreme Court of Ohio ("Ohio Board"), decided very recently in Opinion 99-9 that based on the situation before it, lawyers could practice law by using e-commerce, through interaction with clients exclusively on the Internet. Specifically, the Ohio Board found that a law firm could charge a fee for receiving and replying to e-mail questions from new clients that sent those questions on an intake form on the law firm's website. At least in Ohio, it is possible to practice law online without ever seeing your client.

The facts presented to the Ohio Board were limited to an intake form on the firm's website that provided for the prospective client's name, address, credit card information, legal question and password for the attorneys to use when replying. The attorneys would disclose that they were only answering based on Ohio law and a flat fee would be charged for a single topic question. The attorney reserved the right to decide if more than one topic was implicated by the question and would also communicate by e-mail if more data were needed before the question could be answered. The facts presented to the Ohio Board did not include any "real time"

communication nor was there any telephone or in-person communication between the attorney and the client.

The reasoning of the Ohio Board in approving e-commerce as a means of practicing law included an emphasis on the need to provide access to legal services, citing Rule 1.1 of the Ohio Code of Professional Responsibility which states that: "[a] basic tenet of the professional responsibility of lawyers is that every person in our society should have ready access to the independent professional services of a lawyer of integrity and competence."

Curiously, the Ohio Board only seven years earlier considered and approved what was at the time a novel idea of delivering legal services by phone to one whom the attorney had no prior relationship. See Ohio Opinion 92-10. *See also* Ohio Opinion 94-27 (approving representation of clients by attorney with physical disability exclusively through contacts with an online-service.)

The Ohio Board noted that any method of legal representation must conform with ethical guidelines, and concluded that attorneys may provide online legal representation by answering e-mail questions from non-lawyers if they follow the following nine ethical conditions:

1. The representation must be free from conflicts of interest. Thus, a conflict check must be done before any legal service is provided and the online intake form should provide enough detail for a conflicts check to be made before any reply to the e-mail is given.

2. All the traditional duties that a lawyer owes a client apply to online legal services, including the need to act competently.

3. The confidence of "e-mail clients" must be protected. In Ohio and in most states, this does not require encryption in most instances. *See* Ohio Opinion 99-2.

4. Advertising of online services must comport with existing advertising rules.

5. No trade names can be used. Rather, the law firm name must be used.

6. The provision of online legal services cannot be a joint enterprise with a non-attorney.

7. An attorney cannot charge an excessive fee for online legal services.

8. The attorney should notify the e-mail client if the e-mail question cannot be answered. Nor may the attorney recommend himself or herself or anyone in the law firm unless the e-mail client asks for advice regarding employment of a lawyer.

9. The attorney must not practice law in a jurisdiction where to do so would violate the ethical rules in that jurisdiction.

The Ohio Board was aware of contrary findings in Arizona at the time it made its decision. See Opinion 97-04 (1997) of the State Bar of Arizona (concluding that prospective clients should not be able to send completed intake forms online due to the "possibility of inadvertent disclosure"). *Cf.* Virginia Formal Opinion A-0110, April 14, 1998 (limiting solicitation in "real time" online chat rooms to the same extent restrictions on solicitation apply to in-person and telephone solicitation.)

In sum, it appears that there is at least one state that has given its imprimatur to lawyers who use e-commerce to enhance their law practice. However, depending of the particular details of how one applies e-commerce to the practice of law in the future, the same familiar limitations on advertising generally, and in-person solicitation, should be used as guidelines. ∎

Francis G.X. Pileggi is the managing partner at the Wilmington, DE office of Manta & Welge. He is a frequent lecturer on topics that include issues of professionalism and ethics. Mr. Pileggi is a national member of the American Inns of Court.

Attorneys and the Internet: Which Ethics Rules Govern?

Francis G.X. Pileggi, Esquire

The legal profession often lags behind other segments of professional society where technological advancements are concerned. Nevertheless, the profession has embraced wholeheartedly the integration of the Internet into its world. The Internet's impact on the legal profession can be felt on four different levels: the use of attorney/firm websites, which provide descriptions of services, expertise, etc.; the use of the Internet to operate a law practice either entirely or predominantly online; the use of real-time chatrooms and bulletin boards to provide online legal advice; and the use of online attorney directories and referral services.

As the rise of state ethics opinions regarding these attorney Internet uses reflects, each use raises questions regarding applicable ethics rules. Currently, the American Bar Association's Ethics 2000 Commission is considering the revision of several ethics rules on advertising to cover some forms of attorney Internet usage.[1] Proposed Model Rule 7.2 would bring attorney websites into the ambit of the advertising rules already in place. If approved, Comment 3 to Rule 7.2 would specifically permit the use of attorney websites for advertising purposes. Proposed Model Rule 7.3 would prohibit the use of real-time electronic contact, e.g., an Internet chatroom, to solicit clients based on the reasoning that the interactivity of the real-time chat poses the same threats as live telephone communication which is already restricted under the Rules.

One overarching issue that clouds any and all ethics questions raised by the various attorney Internet uses is which state or states' ethics rules apply in a given situation. This issue is important as ethics rules differ from state to state. Namely, to be in compliance with state ethics rules in State A does not guarantee compliance with State B's rules. The Internet is a vast network whose information reaches worldwide, thereby potentially exposing an Internet user to any jurisdiction, anywhere in the world. This concern is particularly great for attorneys, who must be sure to abide not only by the criminal and civil laws of a given jurisdiction, but also by the legal ethics rules as well.

No broad consensus has emerged as to which state or states' ethical rules should apply to Internet interactions. Generally, an attorney must abide by the ethics rules of the state in which he or she is licensed to practice. More complex questions arise, however, when the attorney contacts or is contacted by residents of a state in which he or she is not licensed to practice. The probability of this interaction is magnified by the use of Internet communications, particularly through the use of chatrooms and bulletin boards. Among other issues, this situation raises questions of the unauthorized practice of law, which will be discussed later.

One commentator has suggested that the three most important factors in determining which state's rules govern attorney Internet use are the following: (1) the states in which the attorney is admitted to practice; (2) the states in which the attorney is seeking clients; and (3) the states in which the attorney, in fact, practices.[2] A reasonable solution, therefore, seems to require attorney compliance with the ethics rules of those states targeted by his or her Internet use within the scope of his or her practice. The same commentator, however, feared that compliance would be difficult for larger firms as they target a wide market and would potentially be required to comply with many states' ethics rules.

Another option yet to be explored is the drafting of a universal code of attorney Internet ethics rules, giving jurisdiction to a cyberspace location to adjudicate attorney Internet ethics violations. Of course, many concerns regarding any such drafting would arise, including the identities of the drafters and the ratification process. The World Intellectual Property Organization, an intergovernmental organization formed to settle international disputes concerning intellectual property claims, could serve as a model for any such drafting and adjudicating organization.

Whichever state's or states' ethics rules apply to attorney uses of the Internet (assuming a definitive answer is possible), one must next address the specific questions raised by each of the four different attorney uses of the Internet outlined above. The following sections will provide a brief overview of the ethics concerns that states and, in some instances, the ABA have addressed as a result of the integration of the Internet into the practice of law.

The Use of Attorney/Firm Homepages

The use of attorney/firm homepages raises a variety of ethical concerns with most centering on the rules governing the communication of legal services, namely advertising and solicitation. Presently, a few states refer specifically to electronic media and restrict significantly advertising in it.[3] As stated above, the ABA Ethics 2000 Commission is considering a proposed change to Model Rule 7.2 that would include in its comment the approval of websites for advertising purposes. If approved, revised Rule 7.2 would bring attorney homepages into the category of advertisements, thus subjecting the websites to rules concerning advertising located in Section 7 of the Model Rules. Section 7 includes prohibitions on material misrepresentations of fact, communications that create unjustified expectations, and the comparison of the attorney's services with that of another.[4]

Several states have made clear that attorney homepages are within the scope of ethics rules on advertising.[5] Florida, for example, has adopted regulations on attorney homepages into its ethics rules. Under Florida Rule 4-7.6(b), an attorney or firm homepage must include all jurisdictions in which the attorney(s) are licensed to practice and one or more bona fide office locations of the attorney or firm. Although the World Wide Web sites are exempt from filing requirements required of other types of advertising, attorney homepages remain subject to other Florida advertising rules.

The Use of the Internet to Practice Online

The attorney's use of the Internet to practice law either predominantly or entirely online has spurred at least two state ethics opinions approving of the practice so long as other ethics rules are followed. In Opinion 94-27, South Carolina permitted a physically-disabled attorney to operate an "electronic law office." The committee found that operating a law office via electronic media did not, by itself, violate any ethics rules. The committee did point out, however, that an e-attorney must abide by all other ethics rules, including but not limited to those regulating advertising and solicitation, conflicts of interest, and confidentiality.

More recently, in Opinion 99-9, the Board of Commissioners on Grievances and Discipline for the Supreme Court of Ohio permitted Ohio attorneys to operate a law practice through interaction with clients exclusively on the Internet. The Board based its decision on the rationale that "[a] basic tenet of the professional responsibility of lawyers is that every person in our society should have ready access to the independent professional services of a lawyer of integrity and competence."

The Use of Chatrooms and Bulletin Boards to Provide Online Legal Advice

Chatrooms provide an opportunity for online users to communicate live one-on-one with an attorney while bulletin boards allow online users to post legal questions to which an attorney can provide an answer, not in "real-time." The ABA/BNA Lawyers' Manual on Professional Conduct recently listed some ethical concerns that arise in an attorney's use of chatrooms and bulletin boards, including the potential formation of an attorney-client relationship, the potential for the unauthorized practice of law, the potential for conflicts of interest, and the potential for inappropriate fee-splitting with other practitioners.[6] As stated above, the ABA Ethics 2000 Commission has recommended the prohibition of online chatrooms to solicit clients, reasoning that the interactivity of the real-time chat poses the same threats as live telephone communication.

Although most of these virtual legal communities include a disclaimer warning that no attorney-client relationship is created and/or that the information provided is not a substitute for an attorney's advice, many commentators warn that the "boilerplate

disclaimers" attached to the advice may convince courts that an attorney-client relationship has been created.[7] Explaining that giving legal advice in response to specific factual circumstances is "at the heart of the practice of law," Villanova University law professor Catherine J. Lanctot concluded that online chats are sufficient to create an attorney-client relationship when the legal advice is given in response to a particular factual situation.[8] The ABA/BNA Lawyers' Manual on Professional Conduct includes several attorneys' concurring opinions that an attorney-client relationship is likely formed in a chatroom/bulletin board discussion despite broad disclaimers.

Another concern with chatrooms and bulletin board discussion involves the unauthorized practice of law. Questions of jurisdiction arise here as it is unclear as to whether an attorney may advise clients in a state in which he is not licensed to practice without engaging in the unauthorized practice of law. As the Internet is accessible anywhere in the world, the possibility that an attorney may respond to a question outside the state in which he is licensed to practice is great. One commentator has suggested that the best solution for this problem would be a national one as an individually state-driven result may be a piecemeal, inconsistent product.[9]

The potential for conflicts of interest is also great with the use of online chats and bulletin boards. In Opinion 97-04, Arizona warned that the inability to screen for a potential conflict with existing clients and the possibility of disclosing confidential information should steer attorneys away from answering specific legal questions posed in an online chat. Accordingly, attorneys must be cautious concerning the receipt of confidential information.

As nonlawyers may be in business with a lawyer in the operation of chatrooms and bulletin boards, inappropriate fee-splitting with nonlawyers may also be a concern. The ABA/BNA Manual provides the sentiments of several commentators anticipating this problem. The Manual also points out, however, that with the possibility that multidisciplinary practices may be approved, the issue may resolve itself.

The Use of Legal Directories and Referral Services

The use of legal directories and referral services raise concerns similar to those raised in the use of attorney/firm homepages in that rules concerning advertising and solicitation are implicated.

While one state has opined that the participation in a particular referral service is a violation of ethics rules,[10] at least one other state's bar association is planning to introduce an online referral service next year. Early in 2001, the Pennsylvania Bar Association plans to place its lawyer-referral system, one of the oldest in the country, online.[11]

The Internet has virtually invaded the practice of law. The ABA's consideration of ethics rules revisions to cover attorney Internet use in chatrooms and homepages reflect this invasion. While this guidance will be helpful, the use of the Internet in law practice will only expand with time. ∎

Mr. Pileggi is a partner in the Wilmington, Delaware office of Manta and Welge. The substantial research and writing assistance of a summer law clerk of our firm, Michelle Kaminsky, is gratefully acknowledged.

---

[1]The Ethics 2000 Commission is the group charged with reviewing and revising the current Model Rules of Professional Conduct. *See* the America Bar Association's website link to the Ethics 2000 Commission at http://www.abanet.org/cpr/ethics2k.html (outlining all proposed rules and rule changes to be considered by Ethics 2000).

[2]*See* William E. Hornsby, Jr., "Ethics Rules for Ads May Cover Web Sites", *National Law Journal*, January 29, 1996, at C1 (providing advice for attorneys who advertise via the internet).

[3]*See, e.g.*, Calif. Bus. & Prof. Code 6157 et seq. (regulating attorney advertising in electronic media); Iowa DR 2-101 (restricting attorney advertising in electronic media).

[4]See *Model Rules of Professional Conduct Rules 7.1-7.5.*

[5]*See, e.g.*, New York Ethics Opinion 98-2 (1998) (finding that firm website was akin to solicitation and therefore subject to advertising rules); Alabama Ethics Opinion RO-96-07 (1996) (advising that attorney websites are subject to the rules of advertising); Illinois Ethics Opinion 96-10 (1996) (likening attorney websites to the Yellow Pages, thereby subjecting websites to advertising rules).

[6]Joan C. Rogers, "Cyberlawyers Must Chart Uncertain Course in World of Online Advice", *ABA/BNA Lawyers' Manual on Professional Conduct*, March 15, 2000.

[7]*Id.*

[8]Catherine J. Lanctot, "Attorney-Client Relationships in Cyberspace: The Peril and the Promise", 49 *Duke LawJournal* 147, 193 (1999).

[9]See Rogers *supra* note 6.

[10]*See* Arizona Ethics Opinion 99-06 (1999) (advising that an attorney cannot ethically participate in internet service that sends legal questions from individuals to attorneys based on subject matter of question).

[11]*See* Emilie Lounsberry, "The Law Takes to the Internet", *The Philadelphia Inquirer*, June 23, 2000, at C1.

Ethical Referral of Fees Among Lawyers

Francis G.X. Pileggi, Esquire

A lawyer may ethically give another lawyer in a different firm a referral fee subject to compliance with the particular state's ethical rules that govern. In any treatment of an issue such as this one, we must acknowledge that most states have their own slightly unique version of the ethical rules governing referral fees.

For example, in Delaware, Rule of Professional Conduct 1.5(e) provides that "A division of fee between lawyers who are not in the same firm may be made only if: (1) the division is in proportion to the services performed or by written agreement with the client, each lawyer assumes joint responsibility for the representation; (2) the client is advised of and does not object to the participation of all the lawyers involved; and (3) the total fee is reasonable.

By comparison, the counterpart rule in Pennsylvania does not include the first condition found in the Delaware rule. Similarly, the California counterpart rule does not have the requirement found at subsection (1) of Delaware Rule of Professional Conduct 1.5 (e) regarding joint responsibility and payment according to services performed.

Recently, the Ethics 2000 Commission issued its Report on the Evaluation of the Model Rules of Professional Conduct. The commission was charged with the monumental task of reviewing the Model Rules adopted by the American Bar Association in 1983 and recommending any updates that may be appropriate due to the many changes in the profession and in society since 1983.

Among its many suggestions, the commission recommended changes to Model Rule 1.5 relating to referral fees. In his introduction to the November 2000 Report of the Commission, the chair of the commission, Delaware Supreme Court Chief Justice E. Norman Veasey, explained that the commission was recommending that fees for referrals "be permitted without division of work or 'joint responsibility' as long as the total fee is reasonable and the client agrees in a signed writing to the participation of all lawyers involved, including the share of the fee for each lawyer." This recommendation, if followed, would eliminate the requirement found in subsection (1) of Delaware Rule 1.5(e). *See* www.abanet.org/cpr/e2k-final_rules2.htm.

Notably, the commission also suggested that the requirement of a "writing" be satisfied in a manner consistent with recent legislation recognizing the validity of electronic signatures. The commission did not intend to address the issue of fees split by an attorney and a former firm with whom that lawyer was associated.

In the Reporter's notes explaining the proposed changes to Rule 1.5(e), it was made clear that the original intent of the rule was preserved in that it was designed to benefit clients by encouraging better and perhaps more qualified service to a client that could not be provided by the original attorney whom the client contacted. It was also observed that proportioning work and assigning "joint responsibility", as required in the original Model Rule 1.5, was not easily managed and might be contrary to the intent of the rule to encourage the transfer of a matter to a more qualified attorney without continuing involvement by the original attorney.

It should be noted in passing that in some class action and derivative cases, it is not uncommon for attorneys to apportion fees that have been approved in a lump sum by the court, among the different attorneys representing different plaintiffs, without a scientifically precise accounting of the time spent by a particular attorney on specific aspects of the case.

In sum, attorneys in different firms ethically may continue give referral fees to each other. The Ethics 2000 Commission has endorsed a continuation of this practice by proposing a change in the Model Rules that is less restrictive. First, however, check the current version of the ethics rules in your controlling jurisdiction. ■

Francis G.X. Pileggi practices in Wilmington, Delaware with Manta and Welge. He writes and lectures frequently on business law and ethics issues. His e-mail address is francis.pileggi@mantalaw.com.

Recent Ohio Decision Restricts Content of Law Firm Websites

Francis G.X. Pileggi, Esquire

The applicability of traditional rules of professional conduct to law firm websites was recently clarified in Ohio. In a recent decision, the Board of Commissioners on Grievances and Discipline for the Supreme Court of Ohio (the "Board") decided that it was a violation of the Ohio Code of Professional Responsibility for a law firm to use client quotations on the homepage of the law firm website. *See* Board Opinion 2000-6 (December 1, 2000). The quotations were general statements from existing clients regarding the law firm's service, responsiveness, and style, although they did not describe any particular transaction or litigation matter that the firm has handled or is currently handling. The client would be identified by name and company. The opinion was based on a proposed set of facts and not an existing violation.

The Board relied on Ohio Code of Professional Responsibility Rule 2-101(A)(3) that provides in part that "a lawyer shall not comment on his or her own behalf or that of a partner, associate, or other lawyer affiliated with the lawyer's firm; use, or participate in the use of any form of public communication, including direct mail solicitation that: contains any testimonial of past or present clients pertaining to the lawyer's capabilities." The Board also relied on DR 2-101(C), that provides in part that "a communication is false or misleading if it satisfies any of the following:…is subjectively self-laudatory, or compares a lawyer's services with other lawyers' services, unless the comparison can be factually substantiated."

Also found relevant was DR 2–103(C) which generally prohibits a lawyer from asking a person or organization to recommend or promote the use of a lawyer's services. DR 2-101(A)(3) does not define "testimonial", but the Board referred to the dictionary definition to determine what was prohibited and found that "a testimonial includes objective statements of truth or fact as well as subjective affirmation of worth or character." The Board held that the statements at issue were an affirmation of the character of the lawyers within the firm and were therefore prohibited under Ohio Code of Professional Responsibility DR 2-101(C)(3). Opinion 2000-6 at 3.

Although not adopted in Ohio, the Board also referred to ABA Model Rule 7.1 which prohibits client testimonials. The Model Rule describes them as client endorsements. The comment to ABA Rule 7.1, relied on by the Board, provides that "the prohibition…[against] statements that may create unjustified expectations would ordinarily preclude advertisements about results obtained on behalf of clients, such as the amount of a damage award or the lawyer's record in obtaining favorable verdicts and advertisements containing client endorsements".

The Board had previously issued an opinion prohibiting advertisements that contain client testimonials. *See* Opinion 89-24. In Opinion 89-24, the Board reasoned that an attorney cannot effectively avoid the ban on self-laudatory statements by having a client rather than the attorney, make such statements.

The Board concluded that a client's quotations on a firm website about the general nature of the legal services provided, the responsiveness of the law firm, and other non-substantive aspects of the firm's representation is a violation of the Ohio Professional Rules of Conduct. Opinion 2000-6 at 5. Thus the Board advised the law firm to avoid client testimonials regarding the quality of the law firm's services that cannot be verified by reference to objective standards, as well as those that involve the lawyer or law firm recommending that the client promote the law firm's services to others. *Id.* This recent ethics opinion is an example of the need to review the traditional rules regarding advertising when firm websites are being designed. ■

Francis G.X. Pileggi, Esq. is a partner in the Wilmington, Delaware office of Fox, Rothschild, O'Brien & Frankel, LLP. He often writes on issues of ethics and business law.

Court Decides that Rule of Professional Conduct 5.6 Does Not Apply in Dispute Over Lawyers's Employment Contract

Francis G.X. Pileggi, Esquire

A recent decision by the U.S. Court of Appeals for the District of Columbia Circuit held that Rule of Professional Conduct 5.6 does not invalidate a liquidated damages provision in a lawyer's employment contract with his former law firm. In *Ashcroft & Gerel v. Coady*, 244 F.3d 948 (D.C.Cir. 2001), the Court of Appeals affirmed the District Court's judgment in favor of a law firm whose attorney breached his employment contract by, *inter alia*, allegedly stealing clients, conspiring with other attorneys to defraud the firm and sabotaging firm computers, specifically finding that Rule of Professional Conduct 5.6 – which prohibits agreements restricting the right of attorneys to practice after leaving a firm – did not apply. *Id.* at 955.

In order to understand the decision, a summary of the details is needed. Coady was an attorney with Ashcroft & Gerel from 1989 to 1998. In early 1997 a dispute arose between Coady and Ashcroft & Gerel over the law firm's alleged failure to pay him a bonus, a matter which Coady took to arbitration. At the same time, Ashcroft & Gerel sued Coady in District Court for breach of contract, breach of fiduciary duties and conversion. *Id.* at 949. The arbitration panel found in favor of Coady. A District Court upheld the panel's ruling; however, the Court of Appeals reversed, holding that that the panel lacked jurisdiction to consider Coady's breach of contract claim. *Id.* at 950.

The Court of Appeals also transferred Coady's claim to the District Court which was considering Ashcroft & Gerel's claim against him. The jury returned a verdict in favor of Ashcroft & Gerel's breach of contract claim against Coady in the amount of $400,000,

which corresponded with the liquidated damages provision in Coady's employment contract. *Id.*

On appeal, Coady contended (1) that Ashcroft & Gerel's conduct in attempting to deprive him of a bonus was a material breach and so relieved Coady of any obligation to perform his duties under his employment contract; (2) that the District Court wrongfully prevented Coady from introducing certain evidence of Ashcroft & Gerel's material breach; and (3) that the District Court erred in refusing to strike Ashcroft & Gerel's claim for liquidated damages. The Court of Appeals affirmed the District Court as to Ashcroft & Gerel's conduct not relieving Coady of his employment obligations and the propriety of the liquidated damages award. However, the Court of Appeals determined that Coady had been prejudiced by the District Court denying him an opportunity to introduce evidence which might have demonstrated Ashcroft & Gerel's material breach, and so reversed the judgment and remanded the case to the District Court. *Id.* at 956.

Notably, the Court of Appeals upheld the liquidated damages provision in Coady's employment contract, finding that the $400,000 amount was neither unenforceable on public policy grounds nor was it a penalty, inasmuch as the amount set forth in the contract had no relationship to the amount of actual damages. *Id.* at 955. The Court of Appeals concluded otherwise, finding that Coady's employment contract had routinely been amended to increase the amount of liquidated damages as he

became more valuable to the law firm, to a point where Ashcroft & Gerel lost between $1 million and $1.5 as a result of his termination. *Id.*

In his opposition to the liquidated damages award, Coady relied upon District of Columbia Rule of Professional Conduct 5.6, which prohibits a law firm from restricting "the rights of a lawyer to practice after termination of the [employment] relationship." *Id.* The Court of Appeals rejected Coady's argument, concluding that Rule 5.6 "is inapplicable because the liquidated damages were not linked to Coady's decision to compete with the firm." *Id.* The Court of Appeals further remarked that "the terms of the employment contract are readily distinguishable from a contract not to compete." *Id.*

Significantly, the Court of Appeals, finding Rule 5.6 inapplicable, did not defer to trial testimony by an Ashcroft & Gerel partner that the liquidated damages provision was, in fact, designed to penalize attorneys who, upon leaving the law firm, hoped to compete with their former firm. *Id.* Had the Court given this testimony greater deference, it may very well have concluded that Rule 5.6 precluded an award of liquidated damages. In any event, it is foreseeable that cases may come down the road that apply Rule 5.6[1] to similar facts and conclude that a liquidated damages provision, such as that found in *Coady*, violates Rule 5.6.

---

[1] *It should be noted that the ABA Ethics 2000 Commission Report on the Evaluation of the Model Rules of Professional Conduct, a comprehensive study of the Model Rules, did not recommend any substantive changes to Rule 5.6.*

Francis Pileggi is a partner in the Wilmington, Delaware office of Fox, Rothschild, O'Brien & Frankel, LLP.

Recent ABA Opinion Approves Partnerships with Foreign Lawyers

Francis G.X. Pileggi, Esquire

Recently, the American Bar Association issued Formal Opinion 01-423 which interpreted Model Rule of Professional Conduct 5.4 as allowing, under certain conditions, U.S. lawyers to form partnerships or other entities to practice law with foreign lawyers who are partners or owners. The opinion provides limitations and definitions for the types of foreign lawyers that would qualify. Different foreign countries have different standards and categories for lawyers and the opinion requires that for purposes of the arrangement, the foreign lawyer must be a member of a recognized legal profession in a foreign jurisdiction and the arrangement must be in compliance with the law of jurisdictions where the firm practices. Responsible lawyers in a U.S. law firm have ethical obligations to take reasonable steps to ensure that matters in their U.S. offices involving representation in a foreign jurisdiction are managed in accordance with applicable rules of ethics, and that all lawyers in the firm comply with other applicable ethical rules.

The issue presented to the American Bar Association was whether the practice of U.S. lawyers forming partnerships with foreign lawyers violated the Model Rules of Professional Conduct barring formation of law partnerships or similar associations with non-lawyers and the prohibition against sharing legal fees with non-lawyers, or assisting another in the unauthorized practice of law. The ABA committee issuing the opinion found that the Model Rules do not prohibit U.S. lawyers from forming partnerships with foreign lawyers for the purpose of practicing law.

It was observed that Rule 5.4 is directed mainly against entrepreneurial relationships with non-lawyers and is primarily for the purpose of protecting a lawyer's independence and exercising professional judgment on the client's behalf, free from control by non-lawyers. Model Rule 5.4 states in relevant part:

(a) A lawyer or a law firm shall not share legal fees with a non-lawyer, except that:
  (1) an agreement by a lawyer with the lawyer's firm, partner, or associate may provide for the payment of money, over a reasonable period of time after the lawyer's death, to the lawyer's estate or to one or more specified persons;
  (2) a lawyer who purchases the practice of a deceased, disabled, or disappeared lawyer may, pursuant to the provisions of Rule 1.7, pay to the estate or other representative of the lawyer the agreed-upon purchase price; and
  (3) a lawyer or law firm may include non-lawyer employees in a compensation or retirement plan, even though the plan is based in whole or in part on a profiting-sharing arrangement.
(b) A lawyer shall not form a partnership with a non-lawyer if any of the activities of the partnership consist of the practice of law.

(c) A lawyer shall not permit a person who recommends, employs, or pays the lawyer to render legal services for another to direct or regulate the lawyer's professional judgment in rendering such legal services.
(d) A lawyer shall not practice with or in the form of a professional corporation or association authorized to practice law for a profit, if:
  (1) a non-lawyer owns any interest therein, except that a fiduciary representative of the estate of a lawyer may hold the stock or interest of the lawyer for a reasonable time during administration;
  (2) a non-lawyer is a corporate director or officer thereof; or
  (3) a non-lawyer has the right to direct or control the professional judgment of a lawyer.

Currently, the District of Columbia is the only U.S. jurisdiction that allows lawyers to have non-lawyer partners, subject, however, to stringent conditions. Beyond the scope of this article is the related issue of multidisciplinary practice, which, of course, involves lawyers and non-lawyers practicing together.

Opinion 01-423 found support for its reasoning in Model Rule 7.5 which allows the partnership of lawyers licensed in different jurisdictions.

The American Bar Association has recognized in this opinion the desirability of assuring the availability of foreign lawyers to assist clients in the United States with issues involving foreign law, and has furthered the reciprocal opportunities for U.S. lawyers to practice abroad by adopting a Model Rule For The Licensing Of Legal Consultants. See ABA House of Delegates Report 105E, *Summary of Action Taken by the House of Delegates of the American Bar Association*, ABA 1993 Annual Meeting, New York, New York, August 10-11, 1993, 29-34.

The opinion did not attempt to make a rigid definition for "foreign lawyer", but rather acknowledges that it is a factual determination based on the rules and customs and practices of each particular foreign jurisdiction. The focus should be on the types of services provided by the foreign lawyer with the understanding that there are some foreign jurisdictions that do not have a recognized legal profession as we know it. In those countries, the foreign professional would not be ethically permitted to form a partnership with a U.S. lawyer under Rule 5.4.

In sum, the ABA opinion provides an acceptable method for U.S. lawyers, through affiliation with others, to provide more comprehensive legal services that involve representation in a foreign jurisdiction. ▪

Francis G.X. Pileggi, Esq. is a partner in the Wilmington, Delaware office of Fox, Rothschild, O'Brien & Frankel, LLP. He often writes on issues of ethics and business law.

Recent Ohio Decision Clarifies Conflict of Interest Rule for Matters Involving Positions Adverse to a Client

Francis G.X. Pileggi, Esquire

In a decision that clarifies the confidentiality and loyalty underpinnings of the conflict of interest principles in Ohio's version of Rule 5-105 of the Code of Professional Responsibility, the U.S. District Court for the Northern District of Ohio very recently ruled that a law firm would not be disqualified from defending a company in litigation when another office of the same firm represented the plaintiff in an administrative proceeding in an unrelated matter. The court reasoned that: "if the attorney can show that he can represent adverse clients concurrently with equal vigor, without conflict of loyalties and without using confidential information to the detriment of either client," the presumption of a conflict in concurrent adverse representation is rebutted. *Pioneer-Standard Electronics, Inc. v. Cap Gemini America, Inc.*, No. 1:01 CV 2185, at 7 (N.D. Ohio, March 11, 2002).

The factual background that gave rise to the conflict issue involved Pioneer-Standard Electronics, Inc. ("Pioneer"), a distributor of electronics and computer products, who hired Cap Gemini America, Inc. (Cap Gemini"), a consulting firm, to modify Pioneer's software. A dispute arose regarding that engagement, and Pioneer sued Cap Gemini. Cap Gemini retained Shearman and Sterling to defendant it in the lawsuit filed by Pioneer. Shearman, however, was representing Pioneer in an unrelated regulatory matter, from a different office that was handling the litigation.

Although Shearman terminated its relationship with Pioneer after Pioneer refused to waive the conflict, the court analyzed the case as one of concurrent litigation. Pioneer moved to disqualify Shearman from the Cap Gemini lawsuit based on Rule 5-105 (B) of the Ohio Code of Professional Responsibility that prohibits an attorney from "multiple employment if the exercise of his independent professional judgment on behalf of a client is likely to be "adversely affected" by his representation of another client."

The court found that a law firm could not convert an existing client into a former client simply by a self-serving, unilateral withdrawal, and therefore the "substantially related" test that governs former client conflicts was not applicable. Rather, the conflict among existing clients must be analyzed under the stricter test for concurrent adverse representation. The court determined that the stricter test for concurrent representation is not a per se rule against an attorney representing clients adverse to each other, but rather it creates a rebuttable presumption. *Id.* at 6-7.

The court made a factual finding that there was no confidential information that the Shearman firm could use from its representation of Pioneer in a separate matter, against Pioneer in the defense of Pioneer's claim against a different Shearman client. The court also found that there was no barrier to the Shearman firm pursuing both the defense of the litigation opposing Pioneer's claim and a separate, unrelated regulatory matter on behalf of Pioneer, simultaneously with equal vigor.

Judge Patricia Gaughan reasoned that the factually determinative factor in her analysis was that the two separate matters were being handled by separate lawyers in separate offices of the Shearman firm and that the regulatory matter and the lawsuit were wholly unrelated. The court noted that the result would have been the same under Model Rule of Professional Conduct 1.7 rather than DR 5-105 of the Model Code of Professional Responsibility. *Id.* at 8 n.3

Judge Gaughan was persuaded by the logic of the decision in *Elonex I.P Holdings, Ltd. v. Apple Computer, Inc.*, 142 F. Supp.2d 579 (D. Del. 2001), which was based on Rule 1.7. In the *Elonex* case, the Dechert firm represented Apple in one suit and also represented Elonex in a separate suit that named Apple as a defendant. Both matters, however, were unrelated and the court found that there was no likelihood of passing confidential data between Apple and Elonex. *Id.* at 582. Thus, the court concluded that Dechert "could reasonably serve both clients' interests." *Id.*

This decision is an example of one possible situation where a law firm can be on the opposite side of a case taking an adverse position against one of its clients, at the same time it is advocating on behalf of that same client in an unrelated matter. Of course this analysis of the ethical rules does not address various related practical concerns of client relations, such as when a firm represents more than one client in the same industry. ■

Francis G.X. Pileggi, Esq. is a partner in the Wilmington, Delaware office of Fox, Rothschild, O'Brien & Frankel, LLP. He often writes on issues of ethics and business law.

Congress Passes New Ethics Rule for Lawyers

On July 25, 2002, the United States Congress passed, and on July 30, 2002, President Bush signed, the Sarbanes-Oxley Act of 2002 which is a broad ranging effort to impose additional responsibility and penalties regarding the conduct of officers and directors of public companies, as well as professionals who advise them. Section 307 of the Act created a new rule of professional responsibility for attorneys "appearing and practicing" before the Securities and Exchange Commission ("SEC") "in any way in the representation of" publicly held companies. Supplanting the traditional role of each state to regulate the attorneys in each state, the Act requires the SEC to enact rules within 180 days to set forth "minimum standards of professional conduct for attorneys," including the following two rules:

> 1) Requiring an attorney to report evidence of a material violation of securities law or breach of fiduciary duty or similar violation by the company or any agent thereof, to the chief legal counsel or the chief executive officer of the company (or the equivalent thereof); and

> 2) If the counsel or officer does not appropriately respond to the evidence (adopting, as necessary, appropriate remedial measures or sanctions with respect to the violation), requiring the attorney to report the evidence to the audit committee of the board of directors of the issuer or to another committee of the board of directors comprised solely of directors not employed directly or indirectly by the issuer, or to the board of directors.

The regulation of attorneys' professional conduct by Congress, and the SEC, instead of the individual states, was not quite as onerous as the new board that the Act established for oversight of the accounting profession, which in many ways brings to an end the self-regulation of the accounting profession. Nonetheless, it will be necessary to be aware of, and novel to watch, how the SEC will prepare rules of professional conduct within 180 days, compared to the work product proposed by the commission of the American Bar Association recently, that updated the Model Rules of Professional Conduct, after several years of analysis, scholarly debate and commentary by the best of our profession. Of course, even those new rules, once approved by the ABA, must be adopted by each state, a process that often takes many more years.

The interface between the ABA Model Rules of Professional Conduct with Section 307 of the Act, can be seen with Rule 1.13 of the rules of professional conduct, which deals with the "organization as client." Rule 1.13 of Delaware's Rules of Professional Conduct, provides that if a lawyer for an organization knows that an officer or employee or other person associated with the organization is engaged in a violation of law, the lawyers shall proceed "in the best interest of the organization." However Rule 1.13 does not require that the attorney report such wrongdoing to the same extent as Section 307 of the Act. Rather Rule 1.13(b) provides that the measures taken shall be "designed to minimize disruption of the organization and the risk of revealing information relating to the representation to persons outside the organization." Rule 1.13(b) provides three suggestions for attorneys in this situation, which include referring the matter to the board of directors, but does not require it. Moreover, Rule 1.13(c) gives the option to a lawyer of simply resigning his or her representation in this situation.

The interplay of Section 307 of the Act with Rule 1.6 of the rules of professional conduct is also instructive. Rule 1.6(b) of Delaware's Rules of Professional Conduct provides that a lawyer "may" reveal confidential information to the extent that the lawyer reasonably believes necessary to prevent the client from committing a criminal act "that the lawyer believes is likely to result in imminent death or substantially bodily harm …" Presumably, no matter how sinister or nefarious, the types of securities law violations that seem to be the focus of section 307 of the Act, would, generally speaking, not likely be the type of criminal act that would result in imminent death as referred to in Rule 1.6.

In any event, while the American Bar Association is in the process of adopting a new and updated revision of the Model Rules of Professional Conduct for minimum standards of professional behavior required by attorneys, after an appropriate deliberative period of years of analysis and debate, the United States Congress has in a matter of weeks preempted the states and imposed its own professional conduct rules on attorneys, at least in a limited area involving publicly held companies. Although it often takes several years for all 50 states to consider adoption of the ABA's model rules, Congress has given the SEC a mere 180 days to issue rules pursuant to the two principles of attorney governance enacted in Section 307. All attorneys should be interested in the result of the SEC's work product that is due within 180 days of the Act's effective date. ◆

Francis G.X. Pileggi, Esq. is a partner in the Wilmington, Delaware office of Fox, Rothschild, O'Brien & Frankel, LLP. He often writes on issues of ethics and business law.

Proposed Ethics Rule by Securities and Exchange Commission Breaks New Ground in Federal Regulation of Attorney Conduct

On November 21, 2002, the Securities and Exchange Commission firmly established itself as a major player in creating standards of attorney conduct and enforcement of ethical standards for lawyers. In a 93-page release, the SEC issued a proposed rule regulating the professional conduct of attorneys—even those who do not "formally" appear before the SEC in the traditional sense. The 93-page document answered a mandate from Congress included in Section 307 of the Sarbanes-Oxley Act of 2002.

Numerous scholarly articles will undoubtedly be written on the many issues raised by this proposed rule, but the limited space allowed for this column will confine me to a brief commentary on the proposed rule and the SEC's explanation included in the 93-page publication by the SEC ("SEC" or "Commission").

As an introductory note, one of the striking aspects of this far-reaching document is the celerity with which it was issued. In barely 3 ½ months, the SEC wrote a rule establishing ethical standards for lawyers. By comparison, a select group of scholars, appointed by the American Bar Association and headed by Delaware Supreme Court Chief Justice E. Norman Veasey, spent a more appropriate period of several years of deliberation, comment and revisions, for a limited mandate of merely updating the well-established model rules of professional ethics, within the traditional framework of state regulation of attorneys by their respective state courts. By contrast, the Commission, pursuant to Congressional mandate, issued an entirely new proposed ethics rule, allowing less than 30 days for comment, before the rule is expected to become effective in January 2003, the month following the comment deadline.

My very circumscribed focus in this short column will be on two portions of the proposed rule. First, I will address the broad scope of applicability that the proposed rule will have for lawyers. Second, I will briefly comment on the aspect of the proposed rule that in some cases requires a "noisy withdrawal" from representation, not only in instances of a material violation of securities law that is ignored by the corporation, but also for breaches of common law fiduciary duties. It is notable that thousands of court decisions in the State of Delaware alone have been written about the multi-faceted aspects of corporate fiduciary law, and even experts in the area of corporate fiduciary duties often disagree about when a breach has occurred. However, the proposed rule by the Commission would in some instances require an attorney to notify the Commission when merely one lawyer believes that a material violation has occurred and is being ignored.

The broad scope of applicability of the proposed SEC rule is addressed at page 12 of the Commission's Release. Proposed Rule 205.2(a)(5)(ii) makes the rule applicable to attorneys who advise any party that the party "is not obligated to submit or file a registration statement ... or other document with the Commission or its staff." This quoted language could reasonably be read to apply to an attorney who, at least by implication, advises a group of two or three persons who are forming a corporation that the issuance of shares to them by the corporation need not involve a registration statement or other filing with the SEC. Therefore, a large number of business lawyers who do not regularly represent publicly-held companies and whose practice involves the formation of companies for small groups of qualified investors could arguably be subject to the requirements of this new SEC rule. For example, if two brothers want to form a new company and are the sole shareholders of that new company, their lawyer would ordinarily advise those brothers that the issuance of shares to them by the corporation they are forming does not require the filing of a registration statement with the SEC. The quoted portion of the proposed rule would arguably be applicable nonetheless, because the attorney advised those brothers that they need not file a registration statement.

The stated purpose of the new Rule 205.1, found on page 70 of the Release, limits the scope to attorneys who represent "an issuer" of publicly traded stock. The actual text, however, of proposed Rule 205.2(a)(5)(ii) does not limit its applicability to attorneys representing issuers to the extent that it defines an attorney "appearing before the Commission" to include an attorney who merely advises any party that the party "is not obligated to submit or file a registration statement ... or other document with the Commission or its staff."

Also notable at page 16 of the Release is the emphasis by the Commission that "the [Sarbanes-Oxley] Act does not contain any exemption or other limitation for small entities." The Release does not define "small entities" but merely concludes at page 69 that "it does

Francis Pileggi is a partner in the Wilmington, Delaware office of Fox, Rothschild, O'Brien and Frankel, LLP, and often writes on topics of ethics, professionalism and business law. His e-mail address is fpileggi@frof.com.

not seem necessary or appropriate to develop separate requirements for small entities." As for whether small entities would incur hardship in establishing a "qualified legal compliance committee," the Release simply notes that such QLCCs are not required under the proposed rule.

Proposed Rule 205.3(d) provides that when outside attorneys have made a report to the corporation regarding evidence of a "material violation," and an appropriate response is not received within a reasonable time, and that attorney reasonably believes that the reported material violation is ongoing or is about to occur and is likely to result in substantial injury to the financial interest of the issuer or of investors, outside attorneys are required to withdraw from the representation, notify the Commission of their withdrawal, and disaffirm any submission to the Commission that they have participated in preparing that is tainted by the violation. The required notification to the SEC is referred to as a "noisy withdrawal."

The commentary referred to at page 9 of the Release for a material violation is also exceedingly broad because proposed Rule 205.2(i) defines a material violation to include "a material breach of a fiduciary duty." Likewise, proposed Rule 205.2(d) defines a breach of fiduciary duty to refer to "any breach of fiduciary duty recognized at common law, including, but not limited to, misfeasance, nonfeasance, abdication of duty, abuse of trust, and approval of unlawful transactions." To be sure, there are some breaches of

corporate fiduciary duty that are clear and unambiguous violations, but the case law on corporate fiduciary duty is replete with "close calls" where reasonable people, very well-versed in this area of the law, disagree about whether a particular set of facts constitutes a breach of fiduciary duty. However, the proposed rule would require under certain circumstances an attorney to report what that attorney believes to be a breach of fiduciary duty, even if others might disagree that a breach of fiduciary duty occurred. This will likely make the officers of the corporation with whom the lawyer deals, less likely to disclose confidential information that might force the attorney to reveal such potential breaches.

In closing it should be noted that the foregoing is only a proposed rule and although the period for comment is less than 30 days, when the final version of the rule is promulgated in January 2003, it may be in a different form, at which time more definitive commentary can be made.

For those attorneys who advise shareholders, directors and/or corporations in connection with fiduciary duty obligations, the broad proposed application of the rule implementing Section 307 of the Sarbanes-Oxley Act of 2002 imposes greater liability on the attorney who does not "make a noisy withdrawal" in situations where he is not satisfied with the response of the corporation to the notification of a material breach of either securities laws or of a fiduciary duty. ◆

Ethics and Arbitrators: S.D.N.Y. and Texas Court of Appeals Examine Conflicts of Interest

Two ethics issues involving arbitrators recently have been addressed by a federal district court in New York and the Texas Court of Appeals. The U.S. District Court for the Southern District of New York addressed whether an attorney who served as a party-appointed arbitrator on a three-member panel is allowed, after the arbitral process has been completed, to serve as counsel in a related matter for that party. The court answered in the affirmative. *Feinberg v. Katz*, S.D.N.Y., No. 01 Civ. 2739 (CSH), 2/5/03.

A Texas appellate court upheld a trial court's decision to vacate an arbitration award based on "evident partiality" by the sole arbitrator, concluding that the arbitrator exhibited evident partiality by failing to disclose information that he was under a duty to disclose. Specifically, in a construction defect dispute, he should have revealed that he had an ongoing attorney-client relationship with a trade association of which two of the parties to the arbitration were members. *Houston Village Builders Inc. v. Falbaum*, Tex. Ct. App. 14th Dist., No. 14-01-01105-CV, 1/23/03.

In *Feinberg*, Senior Judge Charles S. Haight, Jr., concluded that because party-appointed arbitrators in a three-arbitrator panel are not impartial or neutral, but rather advocates, New York Code of Professional Responsibility EC 5-20, which prohibits only impartial arbitrators from representing parties, does not apply to disqualify such a non-neutral arbitrator.

The New York case arose after Norman Katz sold his interest in a women's lingerie company to Herbert Feinberg, and the parties disputed the calculation of the purchase price and alleged fraudulent conduct. The purchase agreement called for all disputes between the parties to be arbitrated by a three-person panel, with each party selecting an arbitrator, and the third arbitrator would be chosen by the two selected arbitrators.

Katz chose Alvin B. Davis of Steel Hector & Davis as his arbitrator, who acted as Katz's advocate during the arbitration proceedings. Once the arbitration was completed, Davis represented Katz in federal and state court in lawsuits brought by Feinberg as well as settlement discussions and a subsequent arbitration with Feinberg.

Feinberg objected to Davis' representation of Katz, seeking to disqualify him from the matter before the district court. Judge Haight rejected all three arguments that Feinberg advanced in favor of disqualifying Davis.

Feinberg relied on New York Code of Professional Responsibility EC 5-20, which prohibits an attorney who

has acted as an "impartial arbitrator or mediator" from representing any of the parties involved in that dispute. The district court determined based on case law that a party-designated arbitrator in a tripartite panel is not impartial within the meaning of EC 5-20. Therefore, since Davis was serving as a party-appointed arbitrator, he could not be considered "impartial" and EC 5-20 did not apply to bar his later representation of Katz in related matters.

Reinforcing his decision were Judge Haight's determinations that both Katz and Feinberg had the right to choose their own arbitrators, no language in the arbitration clause neutralized the partiality of these party-designated arbitrators and this was a commercial dispute. Further, the third admittedly neutral arbitrator stated that the she was the principal author of the arbitration award and the two party-selected arbitrators were understood to be serving in a partisan capacity.

The district court concluded that EC 5-20 does not apply to partisan arbitrators, finding that the adjective "impartial" was a significant modifier of the nouns "arbitrator" and "mediator." Moreover, the court said the ABA Model Rule 1.12(d), although not adopted in New York at the time of the decision; clears up any ambiguity created by EC 5-20 by stating that an "arbitrator selected as a partisan of a party in a multimember arbitration panel is not prohibited from subsequently representing that party."

New York Disciplinary Rule 9-101A also failed to sway the district judge that Davis should be disqualified. DR 9-101A states that a "lawyer shall not accept private employment in a matter upon the merits of which the lawyer has acted in a judicial capacity." Judge Haight noted that arbitrators are not judges and thus the rule was inapplicable.

Lastly, the district court found no appearance of impropriety sufficient to support disqualification of Davis in his continued representation of Katz. The judge said Feinberg failed to make any specific factual allegations that the litigation would be tainted, either because the attorney's ability to represent his client was compromised or that some confidentiality has been breached. The court noted that even if Davis' representation were to cast a shadow of impropriety, the appearance of impropriety alone is insufficient to disqualify counsel.

In the separate Texas case, the Texas Court of Appeals found that an objective observer would believe that the

Francis G.X. Pileggi, Esq. is a partner in the Wilmington, Delaware office of Fox, Rothschild, O'Brien & Frankel, LLP. He often writes on issues of ethics and business law.

lawyer-arbitrator's representation of a trade group to which two of the parties to the arbitration belonged, might create an impression of partiality or bias in the arbitration proceedings, when there was only one arbitrator who was required to be impartial.

Homeowners William and Jennifer Falbaum sued Village Builders after discovering significant foundation problems in the new home they had purchased. As required by the parties' purchase agreement, the dispute was submitted to binding arbitration subject to the Construction Industry Arbitration Rules of the American Arbitration Association (AAA).

The AAA gave the Falbaums and Village Builders a list of ten potential arbitrators with short resumes attached. After each side was given an opportunity to strike three of the ten candidates, the AAA selected an attorney, Stephen Paxson, to be the sole arbitrator. His resume revealed he was a member of the Greater Houston Builders Association (GHBA). He also disclosed to the AAA that both Village Builders and its parent company, Lennar Homes, were also members of the GHBA. He further stated that neither he nor his firm had ever represented Village Builders or Lennar Homes and that he was "unaware of any potential conflict or other disclosures that would need to be made to the parties."

Paxson ruled in favor of Village Builders in the arbitration. When the Falbaums' lawyer learned that, in addition to being a member of the GHBA, Paxson had an attorney-client relationship with the GHBA, the Falbaums filed a motion to vacate the award under the Texas Arbitration Act on grounds of "evident partiality" by the arbitrator.

The trial court granted the Falbaums' motion and vacated the arbitration award. The trial court concluded that the arbitrator's failure to disclose certain information created evident partiality, requiring the court to vacate the award. Under the Texas Arbitration Act, an arbitration award must be vacated if a party's rights were prejudiced by evident partiality by a neutral arbitrator.

In upholding the trial court's decision, Justice Leslie Brock Yates noted that the Texas Supreme Court has held that a prospective neutral arbitrator selected by the parties or their representatives exhibits evident partiality if he or she does not disclose facts that might, to an objective observer, create a reasonable impression of the arbitrator's partiality. Yates said these disclosures are not limited to direct financial or business relationships, but also include all information that might reasonably affect the potential arbitrator's impartiality.

The appellate court observed that Paxson had a long-term attorney-client relationship with the GHBA. Justice Yates said that although Paxson did not have a direct attorney-client relationship with Village Builders or Lennar Homes, his relationship with the GHBA could be compared to that of an arbitrator who represents the parent company of one of the parties to an arbitration. Here, the appeals court said, the arbitrator's representation was personal and ongoing at the time of the arbitration.

Justice Yates wrote, "Furthermore, it is not unreasonable to suggest that someone in the Arbitrator's position might be influenced into ruling in favor of a trade-association member to protect his status as the association's counsel."

The court of appeals applied the test that requires only that an objective observer would believe the undisclosed relationship might create an impression of partiality or bias. The court concluded that the arbitrator's ongoing service as counsel for the GHBA might create a reasonable impression of partiality toward Village Builders and Lennar Homes, two sizable members of that trade association. Accordingly, the court said Paxson was required to disclose the existence of his ongoing attorney-client relationship with the GHBA.

In his dissent, Justice Kem Thompson Frost said the court erred in concluding that the arbitrator exhibited evident partiality by failing to disclose an attorney-client relationship with a trade association that was neither a party nor a witness and whose relationship with the arbitrator could not reasonably have been perceived as creating an impression of partiality in the eyes of an objective observer.

He said that Paxson had no undisclosed connection to any party, lawyer or witness in the arbitration. The "unrevealed information" was an attorney-client relationship between Paxson and the GHBA, a large trade association that was neither a witness nor a party and which had no cognizable interest in the arbitration.

Because the reasonableness of an impression of partiality is dependent on whether the undisclosed information was material, the outcome in this case hinges on the materiality of the Paxson-GHBA attorney-client relationship to the arbitration, Justice Frost argued. He concluded that the relationship in and of itself did not give rise to a reasonable impression of partiality and did not therefore trigger the requirement to disclose the information.

"An objective observer would not attribute any significant influence to an individual member, and thus could not reasonably conclude that two of GHBA's 1350 members could have such weight and influence by virtue of mere membership that the association's lawyer, while serving as an arbitrator in a non-GHBA dispute, might feel compelled to rule for them simply because they are a member," Justice Frost wrote. He cautioned that "casting such a wide net" may result in potential attorney-arbitrators being reluctant to serve, not only because of the breadth of the undertaking and significant potential for error, but also because of the confidential and sensitive nature of peripheral relationships that arguably might fall within the broad net of required disclosures." ◆

ETHICS COLUMN
Francis G.X. Pileggi, Esquire

Wearing Multiple Corporate Hats
Limits Attorney's Access to Discovery Documents

A recent federal court decision supports the view that an attorney who serves as corporate secretary and as a member of the board of directors of a corporation may not have access to plaintiff's "Confidential/Attorney's Eyes Only" discovery materials when acting as co-counsel defending the corporation in litigation. The U.S. District Court for the Northern District of New York addressed in *Norbrook Laboratories, Ltd., v. G.C. Hanford Manufacturing Co.*, (N.D.N.Y., 2003 WL 1956214, April 24, 2003) issues of attorney/client privilege and the duties and obligations of a lawyer to a client, as well as a lawyer/board member to the corporation.

> "... a court should examine the factual circumstances of each individual attorney's relationship to the party demanding access rather than focusing on the attorney's status as in-house or retained. ."

Senior Judge Howard G. Munson found that the defense attorney's dual corporate positions in the defendant corporation created a serious risk of the inadvertent disclosure of plaintiff's confidential documents and information.

Underlying Case
Norbrook Laboratories, Ltd. sued G.C. Hanford Manufacturing Co. (d/b/a/ Hanford Pharmaceuticals), alleging that Hanford misappropriated its trade secrets and confidential information. The companies were direct competitors in the U.S. market for injectable veterinary penicillin products and Norbrook alleged Hanford misappropriated its process for manufacturing a certain type of injectable penicillin.

During discovery, Hanford's co-counsel, Joseph Heath, sought access to Norbrook's documents and information that plaintiff's counsel had designated as "Confidential/ Attorneys' Eyes Only." Heath was also Hanford's corporate secretary and a member of its board of directors. Heath was not "in-house counsel" for Hanford, but rather retained as outside counsel to work on the present litigation.

Norbrook asked the court to deny him access to the confidential material, characterizing Heath's relationship to Hanford as that of an "insider" and arguing that he should not be made privy to Norbrook's trade secret documents.

Heath argued that his duties at Hanford were limited in time and scope in that he attended one monthly meeting of the board of directors in which he prepared the board's minutes. He maintained that his representation of Hanford in the litigation was separate and distinct from his other corporate duties.

District Court Opinion
In reaching his decision, Judge Munson relied on *U.S. Steel Corp. v. United States*, 730 F.2d 1465 (Fed. Cir. 1984), which the court described as the "leading authority on protective orders distinguishing between outside and in-house counsel." He said that in *U.S. Steel* the Federal Circuit Court cautioned against arbitrary distinctions based on the type of counsel employed, noting that in practice the risk of inadvertent disclosure of trade secrets is present with both kinds of counsel.

Judge Munson relied on the *U.S. Steel* court for the reasoning that to evaluate the risk of inadvertent disclosure and whether access to confidential material should be permitted, a court should examine the factual circumstances of each individual attorney's relationship to the party demanding access rather than focusing on the attorney's status as in-house or retained. Accordingly, Judge Munson concluded that whether Heath was Hanson's in-house counsel was irrelevant to his decision.

The Federal Circuit in *U.S. Steel* recognized the phrase "competitive decisionmaking" as a substantial factor in determining whether counsel should be denied access. Judge Munson reasoned that the phrase as used by the Federal Circuit was "shorthand for a counsel's activities, association, and relationship with a client that are as such to involve counsel's advice and participation in any or all of the client's decisions…made in light of similar or corresponding information about a competitor." Judge Munson then found that Heath's dual positions "as corporate secretary and as a member of the board of directors, create a serious risk of inadvertent disclosure of confidential documents and information."

Francis G.X. Pileggi is a partner in the Wilmington, Delaware office of Fox Rothschild LLP and often writes on topics of legal ethics and business law. His e-mail address is: fpileggi@ foxrothschild.com.

The judge observed that while Heath may not have been a direct participant in competitive decisionmaking, as a member of the board of directors, he sat in the same room with those decisionmakers. He concluded that Hanford's board meetings presented an unacceptable opportunity for the inadvertent disclosure of confidential information. He added that while the court did not doubt Heath's assurances he would abide by the protective order, it could not "endorse a situation that places Mr. Heath's ethical obligations as an attorney in direct competition with his fiduciary duty to Hanford."

Accordingly, the court denied Heath's access to Norbrook's confidential materials. Judge Munson noted that Hanford was not unduly prejudiced by Heath's restricted access to materials since co-counsel had been present from the inception of the litigation and was fully versed in the facts and disputes. The court also distinguished this case from that of *U.S. Steel*, where the exclusion of counsel would have forced the party to retain new counsel. ◆

Massachusetts Supreme Judicial Court Clarifies Permissibility of Contact with Former Employees

The Massachusetts Supreme Judicial Court recently interpreted Massachusetts Rule of Professional Conduct 4.2 to allow ex-parte contact with former employees of an adverse party, unless they have retained their own lawyer or have chosen to be represented by the former employer's counsel. *Clock v. Beverly Health and Rehabilitation Services, Inc.*, Mass., No. SJC-08953, (October 29, 2003).

In a case involving a wrongful death action against a healthcare facility, including a claim that a nurse at the facility gave a patient a morphine overdose, the court determined that it was permissible for counsel for the plaintiff to contact a nurse on duty at the time the patient died, when that nurse was not represented by her own counsel. Although the trial court granted a protective order prohibiting plaintiff's counsel from contacting the former employee except in the presence of defense counsel or with prior permission from the court, the plaintiff appealed and the state's high court reversed on an interlocutory appeal basis. The court determined that Rule 4.2 does not apply to former employees. The court reasoned, based on the comments for the version of Rule 4.2 then in effect, that the intent of the rule was not to apply to former employees and by definition ex-employees are not agents of a company within the meaning of the rule.

The current version of Rule 4.2 as adopted by the American Bar Association in February 2002 includes a new Comment 7 which is a revision of the original Comment 4 relied on by the court. The new language provides in relevant part as follows: "Consent of the organization's lawyer is not required for communication with a former constituent." *See generally* L. Fox, "Your Client's Employees Being Deposed: Are you Ethically Prepared?", *Litigation 17* (Summer 2003) (discussing conflict issues if company attorney represents employee in depositions).

The Massachusetts court held that Rule 4.2 existed to protect the attorney/client relationship and that in the context of entities, there was no legitimate interest in preventing the disclosure of unfavorable facts that occurred in the workplace. To conclude otherwise would unfairly tip the balance of the rule in favor of an organization, the court reasoned. The court also noted that the interests of an organization's former employees are not necessarily aligned with those of that organization, and that it cannot be assumed that former employees will be represented by the company attorney.

The Massachusetts Supreme Judicial Court also relied on Comment b of Section 100 of the Restatement of the Law Governing Lawyers, and found that consistent with the weight of authority on the issue. The court also noted that interviewing an adversary's former employee must also comply with Rule 4.1 (duty of truthfulness to third party); Rule 4.3 (dealings with non-represented persons); and Rule 4.4 (use of unfair or illegal tactics to obtain evidence).

This recent decision is of importance to anyone representing businesses and, of course, the version of Rule 4.2 and comments thereto in effect in your jurisdiction, would affect any analysis of this particular issue. ◆

Francis G.X. Pileggi, Esq. is a partner in the Wilmington, Delaware office of Fox Rothschild LLP. He frequently writes on issues of ethics, professionalism and business law. His e-mail address is: fpileggi@foxrothschild.com.

Justice Scalia Clarifies Standards for Recusal

On March 18, 2004, U.S. Supreme Court Justice Antonin Scalia issued a memorandum that explained the reasons why he was denying a motion that he recuse himself. In that memorandum, Justice Scalia clarified the standards of recusal for justices of the U.S. Supreme Court. *Cheney v. United States District Court*, 541 U.S. _____ (2004).

Some may view the decision as peculiar to the special situation that members of the United States Supreme Court find themselves in, to the extent that "substitutes" cannot be appointed in the way that happens when a trial judge or members of many other appellate courts recuse themselves.

Nonetheless, the scholarly and thoughtful analysis of the minutiae of personal relationships and various degrees of friendships among members of the Court and others who may have an interest in cases before the Court, examined how those dynamics related to the standard that would require recusal if "impartiality might reasonably be questioned." 28 U.S.C. § 455(a).

The memorandum noted that recusal of a justice of the U.S. Supreme Court has much more serious consequences than recusal of a trial judge or members of other appellate courts, for example, because recusal of one member of the U.S. Supreme Court could result in a tie vote, thereby preventing the final resolution of important issues, and, in effect, recusal in that situation would be tantamount to a vote in favor of the appellee. Nonetheless, the analysis about what particular personal connections might reasonably raise an issue about impartiality makes this March 2004 decision an important part of jurisprudence regarding the determination of the objectivity of jurists in general.

In sum, Justice Scalia concluded that, based on the circumstances in the specific situation that is the subject of the memorandum, friendship alone of the Vice President was not a ground for his recusal where official action in the Vice President's official capacity was at issue as opposed to his personal fortune or his personal freedom. Justice Scalia described in great detail the many examples in history of justices and presidents of the United States who enjoyed close friendships that did not require their recusal when they were called upon to review official actions of the particular administration or challenges to the actions of a particular president. Justice Scalia provided a more recent example of invitations to the White House for dinner often extended to all of the justices, and a specific invitation extended to the justices and their spouses for a December 2003 Christmas reception at the residence of the Vice President, which included an opportunity for a photograph with the Vice President and Mrs. Cheney.

Justice Scalia found it notable by its absence that the party seeking recusal did not cite a single citation of a justice recusing himself or herself in an "official-action suit," as opposed to instances where the parties involved appeared in their personal capacity. The motion for recusal did not cite a single instance in which a justice either recused himself or was asked to recuse himself based on even remotely similar circumstances as presented in the Cheney case. Rather it seems that the motion for recusal was based almost entirely on newspaper editorials, many of which did not even rely on the correct facts.

Mentioned in passing, but arguably a persuasive part of the reasoning in the memorandum, was the observation that the attorney requesting recusal in the case also happened to be a friend of Justice Scalia who had sent him a "warm note" inviting him to speak at a law school class shortly before the motion for recusal was filed. Justice Scalia noted that the attorney filing the motion sought "to impose, it seems to me, a standard regarding friendship, the appearance of friendship, and the acceptance of social favors, that is more stringent than what they themselves observe." Justice Scalia saw nothing amiss in that friendly letter and invitation but would have thought otherwise if he had applied the standards urged in the motion.

In conclusion, the memorandum clarified that the issue presented was not whether Justice Scalia's personal friendship with the Vice President might cause him to favor the government in a case in which the Vice President was named. Instead, Justice Scalia wrote: "None of those suspicions regarding my impartiality (erroneous suspicions, I hasten to protest), bears upon recusal here. The question, simply put, is whether someone who thought I could decide this case impartially despite my friendship with the Vice President would reasonably believe that I cannot decide it impartially because I went hunting with that friend and accepted an invitation to fly there with him

Francis G.X. Pileggi, Esq. is a partner in the Wilmington, Delaware, office of the law firm Fox Rothschild LLP. He often writes on the topics of ethics, professionalism and business law. His e-mail address is: fpileggi@ foxrothschild.com

on a government plane." Compare generally, *Beam v. Stewart*, Del. Supr., No. 501, 2003 (March 31, 2004) (Delaware Supreme Court addresses whether independence of member of a corporate board of directors should be questioned due to mere personal friendship not of a bias-producing nature).

Justice Scalia concluded by reasoning that: "If I could have done so in good conscience, I would have been pleased to demonstrate my integrity, and immediately silence the criticism, by getting off the case. Since I believe there is no basis for recusal, I cannot."

The careful reasoning and analysis in Justice Scalia's memorandum is destined to be a standard by which personal relationships of judges are measured against their ability to impartially render decisions in cases that come before them. ◆

Has the American Inns of Court Movement Had An Influence on the Legal Profession as a Whole?

CELEBRATING OUR

ANNIVERSARY

By Francis G.X. Pileggi, Esquire

This is a short collection of comments from a select group of members of the bench and bar throughout the country who were asked whether they thought the American Inns of Court movement over the last 25 years has had any impact on the legal profession as a whole in America. This does not purport to be a scientific sampling or a complete cross-section of the legal profession, but rather is intended more in the nature of an anecdotal summary of interviews from people across the country that are familiar with the American Inns of Court, as well as some lawyers that are not involved actively with Inns.

Whatever influence the American Inns of Court movement has had on the legal profession over the last 25 years, we should be able to agree that more work is needed, at least in the area of professionalism. For example, in the July/August 2004 issue of *The Bencher*, Judge Deanell Tacha referred to a *National Law Journal* study that found over 50% of the attorneys surveyed used the word "obnoxious" to describe their colleagues, suggesting a lack of civility is still a problem. A quick review of the latest edition of the *ABA/BNA Lawyers' Manual on Professional Conduct* also supports the view that the legal profession is still in need of much improvement.

From a strictly mathematical point-of-view, with over one million lawyers in the United States and the current members of the American Inns of Court being only about 25,000, less than 10% of the total number of current U.S. lawyers have directly participated in the American Inns of Court (even if alumni of the Inns—which may increase the total to 75,000—are included). Of course it would be hard to measure with precision what the influence of the Inns of Court in America has been, beyond a mere numerical computation, but the sheer statistics dictate less of an influence than that of the Inns of Court counterparts in London where membership is universal and mandatory.

In this collection of anecdotal insights about the influence of the American Inns of Court on the legal profession over the last 25 years, the most practical approach to measure the impact of the Inns of Court is on a geographic basis, not only state by state, but depending on the size of the state, within parts of each state.

Other articles in this issue of *The Bencher* describe in great detail the origin of the American Inns of Court and the goals and principles on which the Inns are based. One of the features of the Inns, in its effort to promote professionalism, civility, competence and collegiality, is the small group nature of the experience promoted by the American Inns of Court. As Dean Robert K. Walsh of Wake Forest University School of Law noted in a Fall 2003 article for the *North Carolina State Bar Journal*, one of the benefits of the small group atmosphere of the Inns of Court is that you get to know other lawyers and judges on a personal level and "it is harder to be uncivil to someone you really know." As U.S. Supreme Court Justice Sandra Day O'Connor was quoted as saying several years ago: "I have been privileged to dine at several Inns of Court, both in London and here in the United States, and to see first hand the healthy interaction of bench and bar, which occurs throughout the year through the mechanism of the Inns. This is an interaction we both need, for we rely on each other a great deal."

The influence of the American Inns of Court on the legal profession varies widely from community to community. For example, in Wilmington, Delaware, Kevin Brady, Esquire, a former trustee of the American Inns of Court, estimates that approximately 50% of the 3,000 or so members of the Delaware Bar (only about 2/3 of whom actively practice in Delaware), have been members—or are members—of the five separate American Inns of Court in that state, at one time or another. On a practical level, Richard DiLiberto, Esquire, a partner at a prominent Delaware firm, recalls interviewing with his current firm while in law school and the chairman (at the time) of his firm, recalling Rick's fine performance during a local Inn program that the chairman had observed. However, Liam Murphy, Esquire, formerly of Wilmington, Delaware, now practicing in a small city in central New York State, observes that the American Inns of Court are hardly known, if at all, where he currently practices.

In the Spring 2004 issue of *Litigation*, the Journal of the American Bar Association's Section of Litigation, Judge Jed Rakoff of the U.S. District Court for the Southern District of New York observes many examples of

declining professionalism and declining ethics especially related to pretrial litigation tactics. He gave the example of two major law firms who paid $51 million and $41 million respectively to settle charges that their reply to a government audit purposely concealed responsive information. *Id.* at 6. He also recounted the case of a partner in a large Chicago firm who billed 6,000 hours a year for each of four years, which worked out to over 16 billable hours per day for 365 days per year. Until he was caught, he was widely admired for his "work ethic." *Id.* Presumably the influence of the American Inns of Court was not sufficient to avoid those examples of problems in the profession; but it is not realistic to expect the Inns to be a panacea.

It may be impossible to eliminate entirely from our profession the lack of civility and lack of professionalism. Regardless of how many American Inns of Court there might be in the future, there will always be lawyers who do not follow the rules and some of them will still succeed, either in spite of—or because of—their hardball tactics. So too, there will always be judges who, either because they do not want to get involved in the policing of pre-trial tactics or do not want to spend the time to deal with it; will "by default" encourage repeat offenders who use Rambo tactics and engage in sharp practices if the net result is that they prevail, especially when engaged in tactics that someone or "the other side," perhaps following the principles espoused by the American Inns of Court, would not want to reciprocate.

Notwithstanding resolutions from the Judicial Conference of the United States as well as the National Conference of Chief Justices and the Judicial Administration Division of the American Bar Association, supporting the ideals and standards promoted by the American Inns of Court, it should not be a surprise that even Inn members, as fallible human beings, can often themselves fail to uphold the highest standards of professionalism and civility.

Judge Carl E. Stewart of the Fifth Circuit Court of Appeals recently observed by phone from Shreveport, Louisiana, that he encourages all of his law clerks to participate in the American Inns of Court. Over the years, this must have a positive influence at least on that group of new lawyers who otherwise would not have had the same "support network" and positive standard of reference early in their careers. Judge Pauline Newman of the U.S. Court of Appeals for the Federal Circuit has observed: "Judges bear a special responsibility for supporting the Inns, not only in

principle but with their time and participation. It is the presence of judges that draws the leaders of the bar, sustaining the vertical integration that is unique to the Inns. And benefits inure to the judges as well as to the practitioners, for we have few occasions to meet together in professional friendship. As a mechanism for preserving the values on which the practice of law was founded, I have come upon no substitute for the Inns of Court."

The insights of those I have interviewed across the country for this article are consistent with the feeling of retired Alabama Justice Hugh Maddox when he stated: "The American Inns of Court is a great organization for the legal profession. I shall always remember the first American Inns of Court conference that I attended in Washington, D.C. The spirit of that meeting caused me to say to myself: 'I am proud to be a lawyer!'" In those communities where an American Inn of Court has infiltrated the legal profession, the views of Bruce Rodger of Media, Pennsylvania, are shared by many. Bruce observed that: "I have personally witnessed the beneficial effects of the American Inns of Court in the community where I practice. The members of our Inn inspire, motivate, educate and support each other, and as a result we are better lawyers, judges and people. Our Inn is not the only organization working for the betterment of our professional community, but it is the best one." That is not to say that members of a particular Inn are immune from engaging in the worst abuses of our profession, but the evidence supports that the risk of such behavior is reduced.

Karen Crawford of San Diego has seen the impact in two different cities as a result of the American Inns of Court movement. She started an American Inn of Court when she moved to Pittsburgh and noticed a profound influence that the membership in the Inns had on those who participated. However, for those lawyers and judges who did not participate, and who did not follow the principles espoused by the American Inns of Court, the continuing challenge for members will always be to "not give in" to the temptation to "reply in kind," to Rambo tactics, even when they appear to succeed and when they are tacitly endorsed by judges who do not penalize that type of behavior. Karen noted how much it helped her in her career by learning from other lawyers and judges and creating bonds in non-adversarial settings.

By "breaking bread" on a regular basis with other lawyers, it reduces the likelihood that you would engage in sharp practices with someone whom you will see on a casual basis frequently and in a professional group that specifically frowns on certain behavior. This should be seen in contrast to the anonymity that may be found in a large bar association in which the likelihood of repeatedly crossing paths with someone more than once is rather remote.

Michael W. Coffield of Chicago, has found that the most notable influence that the American Inns of Court movement has had can be found among smaller firms and younger lawyers. He does not believe that the American Inns of Court have infiltrated larger firms and larger cities as much as it has smaller firms in suburban cities. He notes that the greatest abuses and violations of civility and professionalism are most often noted in pre-trial discovery and deposition tactics, which have a tendency to be more prevalent in larger cities with larger firms and

larger cases in which the stakes may be higher. Mike notes that for almost 20 years since the beginning of the American Inns of Court movement, there was no chapter in Manhattan and he suggests that it may be the nature of the Inn that creates a smaller atmosphere that promotes development of personal working relationships and collegiality, and that makes it more challenging to inculcate into a larger bar association and larger firms.

In sum, even if the influence of the American Inns of Court on the legal profession has been limited, it has had a positive effect, and the more members of the profession who participate in the future, the better our profession will be.

Francis G.X. Pileggi, Esquire is a partner in the Wilmington, Delaware, office of Fox Rothschild LLP. He often writes on issues of ethics and business law. His e-mail address is fpileggi@foxrothschild.com.

Ethical Rules Applicable to Lawyers Forbid Sex with Clients

I must give credit to a colleague for suggesting the topic of this article that one might think was common knowledge or so obvious that it did not merit a separate article. However, anecdotal and other indications support the view that a reminder of this fundamental rule is in order.

Only recently with the adoption of the American Bar Association's Model Rule 1.8(j), based on a recommendation of the Ethics 2000 Commission, which has been enacted in many states, was there a specific rule that flatly prohibited lawyers from having sex with clients. Rule 1.8(j) provides as follows: "A lawyer shall not have sexual relations with a client unless a consensual sexual relationship existed between them when the client-lawyer relationship commenced." I will leave it to others to define "sexual relations" in the context of this rule but Comment 17 to Rule 1.8 explains the rationale behind the rule by noting that a sexual relationship can involve unfair exploitation of a client's vulnerable state that can in turn endanger the lawyer's ability to exercise independent judgment on the client's behalf. This is one example where personal consensual conduct between adults outside of the office is still regulated and can be the basis for substantial penalties.

Comment 17 to Rule 1.8 also takes the position that the rule prohibits an organization's lawyer—whether in-house or outside counsel—from having a sexual relationship with a constituent who supervises, directs or regularly consults that lawyer concerning the organization's legal matters. Thus, this rule also applies to a corporate client. Even when the intimacy preceded the legal representation, related issues can still arise if the romance ends in an unpleasant manner and factual issues arise about applicability of the rule. For example, what if the relevant conduct "stops and then starts again?" The prudent approach would be to avoid any question about the rule's applicability.

Even before the Model Rule explicitly prohibited it, and in states that have not yet adopted Rule 1.8(j), lawyers have been subject to penalties for having such relationships with their clients. See, e.g., ABA Formal Ethics, Op. 92-364 (1992) (citing former Rule 1.8(b) and DR4-101 (B)(2)).

In addition, Model Rule 1.7 applies generally when a "significant risk" exists that the representation of a client will be "materially limited" by a lawyer's "personal interest." Section 125 of the *Restatement of the Law Governing Lawyers* supports the same approach in finding conflicts where there is a "substantial risk" that the representation would be "materially and adversely affected" by the lawyer's "financial or other personal interests." The primary reasoning behind this prohibition barring adverse personal interests is to uphold the primacy of the loyalty that the lawyer owes to the client; and conflicting personal relationships can divide that loyalty and diminish the effectiveness of the lawyer in his or her representation. Rule 1.8(j) furthers that rationale by establishing that the risk of personal gratification prevailing over the best interest of the client should be a temptation that is to be avoided in all cases. See generally *In Re Reynolds*, 515 S.E.2d 927 (S.C. 1999) (lawyer who has sex with a current client's wife violates conflict of interest rules by indulging his personal interests adverse to his client's interests). The personal relationships of a lawyer with people other than a client or his spouse may also raise conflict of interest issues. See, e.g., *Gregory v. Bank of American*, 254 Cal. Rptr. 853 (Cal. Ct. App. 1989) (lawyer who had intimate sexual relationship with opposing counsel's secretary and discussed case with her must be disqualified).

Although it appears that there is a general societal trend toward a separation of the personal life of a professional from an analysis of his professional competence (professional athletes come to mind as an example of this), the foregoing rules and cases illustrate that at least in this area, the regulation of the personal conduct of an attorney "on his own time" is still an aspect of behavior that continues to be subject to careful scrutiny and severe penalties. ◆

Francis G.X. Pileggi, Esq. often writes on issues of legal ethics and business law. He is a partner in the Wilmington, Delaware office of Fox Rothschild LLP. His e-mail address is fpileggi@foxrothschild.com. He is co-chair of the Ethics Subcommittee of the ABA Section of Litigation's Business and Commercial Litigation Committee.

Legal Ethics Now Requires Some Knowledge of Software

A recent decision from the New York State Bar Association Committee on Professional Ethics has interpreted the longstanding obligation of lawyers to maintain the confidences of clients to require also that lawyers guard against the dissemination of "metadata" which can be loosely described as hidden data that is contained in most word processing software and is not generally visible in the hard copy of the document but can be detected in most electronic versions of the document. See 2004 WL 3021157 (N.Y. St. Bar Assn. Comm. Prof. Eth.). The Committee's Opinion Number 782 issued on December 8, 2004 interpreted DR 4-101(B), which provides that a lawyer shall not "knowingly" reveal a confidential secret of a client. The current Model Rules of Professional Conduct provide a similar duty of confidentiality at Rule 1.6(a).

The specific question that was presented to the committee, was whether a lawyer violated the duty to maintain client confidences when that lawyer sent an e-mail that contained attached documents with metadata that reflected client confidences or secrets. Examples of metadata that are often contained in word processing documents include the number of revisions to a particular document; the last ten authors who made revisions to the document; the words and revisions that were deleted or added based on prior versions of the document; comments that were inserted (for example from a client to her attorney); as well as the amount of time spent on the editing of a document. Other information can be obtained depending on the type of document and the type of software that is used. This metadata is usually not visible on the face of the document nor on the hard copy of the document, but can often be obtained if an electronic version of the document is received without the metadata being "cleaned." There are software programs that many firms now use which will "clean the metadata" from any electronic documents attached to e-mails and that one attempts to send. Easily available software packages will prevent the attached electronic document from being sent with the e-mail until the "metadata is cleaned." Based on the decision by the New York State Bar Association Committee on Professional Ethics, it would appear that any attorney sending electronic documents should invest in such "metadata cleaning software" in order to avoid running afoul of one's ethical obligation not to disclose confidential information of a client. Even if the metadata in a document that is sent to opposing counsel does not include comments from a client, it could include confidential work product or other information about prior versions of a document or information about prior clients if the document is a "template" that has been used in other similar representations. The committee's opinion is also based on the assumption that the various exceptions to the rule requiring an attorney to maintain the confidence of a client would not apply.

The committee determined that the requirement of using reasonable care not to inadvertently disclose a client confidence, will vary with the circumstances surrounding the sending of a document by e-mail, such as the subject matter of the document, whether the document has been the subject of multiple drafts with comments from multiple sources and whether the client has commented on the document itself, as well as who the intended recipients of the document might be.

Although lawyer-recipients have an obligation not to exploit an inadvertent or unauthorized transmission of client confidences, a non-attorney recipient would not necessarily have a similar obligation. In a prior opinion by the committee, it found that the use of computer technology to access someone else's client confidences revealed in metadata would constitute an impermissible intrusion on an attorney client relationship in violation of the ethical rules. Absent the use of "metadata cleaning software," other options to avoid transmitting confidential metadata with a document that is e-mailed, would be to convert the document into a pdf format or simply faxing or otherwise sending a hard copy of the document. As an aside, although this short summary is not intended to address electronic discovery issues, the existence of metadata is one reason why many litigators are often more interested in the electronic version of documents than the more conventional hard copy.

In sum, the increased use of technology as a substantial component of law practice today, requires lawyers to be fully conversant with the aspects of software that impact on ethical obligations. ◆

Francis G.X. Pileggi, Esq. often writes on issues of legal ethics and business law. He is a partner in the Wilmington, Delaware office of Fox Rothschild LLP. His e-mail address is fpileggi@foxrothschild.com. He is co-chair of the Ethics Subcommittee of the ABA Section of Litigation's Business and Commercial Litigation Committee.

California Appeals Court allows Expert Hired by Attorney to Sue for Malpractice

The California Court of Appeal, Fourth District, decided in June 2005 that an expert witness being sued by a client may seek equitable indemnity from the law firm that hired him. *Forensis Group, Inc. v. Frantz, Townsend and Foldenaur*, Cal. Ct. App., 4th Dist., No. D044211, June 9, 2005. The case involved the father of the Hernandez family who was killed in a workplace accident when a forklift struck him. The Hernandez family brought a products liability action against the manufacturer of the forklift. Through a referral from the Forensis Group, an expert witness clearinghouse, the law firm retained a mechanical engineer as an expert witness on the products liability claim. The Forensis Group and the expert brought cross-complaints against the law firm for equitable indemnity if they were found liable on a professional malpractice claim. The law firm moved for summary judgment on public policy grounds and the experts appealed.

The California appellate court recognized that "extensive caselaw has addressed the issue of whether an attorney who is sued for malpractice by a former client may cross-complain for equitable indemnity against the successor attorney who has been hired to extricate the client from the condition created by the predecessor attorney. The cases hold that for sound public policy reasons, such cross-complaints are prohibited." (citing *Major Clients Agency v. Diemer*, 67 Cal. App. 1116, 1129 (1998)). The court described this as the "attorney exception" to the general rule allowing indemnity to be sought among joint tortfeasors, as described in *American Motorcycle Association v. Superior Court*, 20 Cal. 3d 578, 598 n. 9 (1978).

The court distinguished the prior cases due to the fact that they dealt with concurrent counsel, as opposed to the expert witness in the expert referral firm who was hired by the client's attorney, to assist in preparing the client's case. The court quoted extensively from the California Expert Witness Guide (Cont. Ed. Bar, 2d ed. 2005). The California Court of Appeals cited Section 8.29 of that Treatise as follows: "An expert is not a mechanical toy that can simply be wound up and turned loose. Regardless of the expert's skill, it is the lawyer's responsibility to make sure that his or her expertise is presented to the trier of fact in an admissible and persuasive way. To accomplish this task, the lawyer needs to understand the substantive details of the expert's testimony and field of expertise."

The court did not find the "attorney exception" to permissible equitable indemnity claims to apply, but held that the trial court erred in ruling that an otherwise permissible equitable indemnification claim was barred by public policy principles. The appellate court found that the prevailing public policy that supported the allowance of a claim against the law firm in this case was "that of protecting the professional interests of all expert witnesses generally to participate in the litigation, and the interests of the judicial system in obtaining the assistance of such expertise. These interests are significant enough to warrant an expert being accorded a right of recourse against those responsible, if any professional negligence should occur on the part of counsel who retain those expert witnesses, with respect to presenting their evidence and defining the proper scope of the experts' duties and obligations within the litigation setting, if any harm to the client should occur. Such a right to recourse for expert witnesses could include equitable indemnity claims." (Slip op. at page 29). Conflict of interest concerns and loyalty and confidentiality issues were summarily set aside as not persuasive reasons to bar the crossclaims by an expert witness against the firm that hired him. The court also noted that the California Supreme Court has found a diminished duty of loyalty toward the former client at least on the part of an attorney who is defending him or herself against an equitable indemnity claim by a fellow litigation professional, in a case arising out of the same client representation (citing California Rule of Professional Conduct 3-310(A)).

In sum, it appears that at least in California, it is not enough to make certain that one's professional conduct as an attorney is both ethical and not vulnerable to claims by clients, but it also appears that attorneys, at least in California, will need to be prepared to defend claims by expert witnesses that they hire if the client is unhappy with a result. ◆

Francis G.X. Pileggi, Esquire is a partner in the Wilmington, Delaware, office of the law firm Fox Rothschild LLP. He often writes on the topics of ethics, professionalism and business law. His e-mail address is: fpileggi@foxrothschild.com. He is co-chair of the Ethics Subcommittee of the ABA Litigation Section's Business and Commercial Litigation Committee.

ETHICS COLUMN
Francis G.X. Pileggi, Esquire

Florida Appellate Court Allows Attorney to Represent Majority Shareholder But Not Corporation

Recently, an appellate court in Florida ruled that despite a conflict that prevented an attorney from representing both the corporation and the majority shareholder in defending derivative and direct claims against the majority shareholder, the same attorney would not be prevented from defending only the majority shareholder. *Campelloni v. Cragan*, Fla. Ct. App. 5th Dist., No. 5D05-1042, Sept. 16, 2005. The court relied on the Florida versions of Rules 1.13 and 1.7. The court acknowledged that Rule 1.13 addresses the issue of dual representation of an organization and a corporate constituent and allows dual representation subject to the provisions of Rule 1.7. Rule 1.7 addresses conflicts with current clients. Rule 1.9 describes duties to former clients. Rule 1.13 covers the multifaceted factual permutations when an organization is the client (or should be the client) as opposed to the constituents of the organization.

The case involved the breakup of three corporations, each of which had only two shareholders. Campelloni and Cragan were shareholders owning 51% and 49% respectively of all the entities. The litigation involved both direct claims and derivative claims in which Cragan made multiple allegations against Campelloni. The trial court disqualified the same attorney from representation of both Campelloni and the corporations. The appellate court reversed.

The appellate court found that the interest of Campelloni and the interest of the corporate entities were not aligned under any construction of the facts alleged. The court also noted that Cragan and Campelloni are the only ones within the entities who could consent to the dual representation, but Cragan did not consent to representation of the entities by the attorney for Campelloni.

Campelloni's attorney, through his dual representation, had access to information regarding the entities, and the trial court determined that Campelloni would have an unfair advantage in the derivative suit if he could use that information against Cragan. That is the basis on which the trial court disqualified Campelloni's attorney from representing either Campelloni or the corporation. The appellate court affirmed the disqualification of Campelloni's attorney for purposes of representing the corporate entities and upheld the trial court's ruling that Campelloni cannot consent on behalf of the corporate entities to the representation by his attorney of the entities. The trial court relied on *Forrest v. Baeza*, 58 Cal. App. 4th 65, 76 (Cal. App. 1997).

The court found that Rule 1.9(a), however, did not support a finding that the prior representation of the corporation by Campelloni's attorney should prevent that same attorney from representing Campelloni in the same case. The court ruled that the implied basis for the complete removal of Campelloni's attorney from the litigation was the trial court's finding that the attorney had access to financial and other information that would give Campelloni an unfair advantage in a derivative action, but the appellate court found that a new attorney would be privy to the same information that Campelloni's current attorney would have in light of Campelloni having access to that confidential information about the corporation in any event.

A key issue in a Rule 1.9 analysis is whether the two client matters are substantially related and whether confidential data was obtained by the lawyer in a prior representation that could be used against a former client. *Compare*, R. Donoghue, *Conflicts of Interest: Concurrent Representation*, 1 Geo. J. Legal Ethics 319, 320 (1998) (party who seeks disqualification under Rule 1.7 need not show any adverse effect from conflict). *See generally, Unanue v. Unanue*, 2004 WL 602096 (Del. Ch.) (director could use long-time corporation attorney to defend him against effort to remove that director by shareholders and other directors -- also, the the court regarded as an important part of its reasoning that it did not find any prejudice to the integrity of the proceedings as a result of the alleged conflict). *See also, Elonex I.P. Holdings, Ltd. v. Apple Computer, Inc.*, 142 F. Supp. 2d 579 (D.Del. 2001) (two offices of large firm were adverse to the same client but were not disqualified under Rule 1.7).

In sum, the ethical rules that apply to representation of shareholders, directors and their entities require a fact-intensive analysis to determine the existence of a conflict, and the starting point is to clarify the identity of any current and prior clients as well as what data was acquired by the attorney that could be used against those clients. When representing an entity, in order to minimize conflict issues, one would be well-advised to clarify at the outset of the representation, in writing, whether the client is the entity or one of its constituents. ◆

Francis G.X. Pileggi is a partner in the Wilmington, DE, office of Fox Rothschild LLP. His e-mail address is fpileggi@foxrothschild.com. He often writes and lectures on issues related to ethics, professionalism and business law. He also maintains a blog at www.delawarelitigation.com.

No Absolute Right to Use One's Surname in Name of Law Firm

The Indiana Supreme Court and the U.S. District Court for the District of Connecticut both addressed very recently the issue of one's right to use one's surname in naming a law firm. The courts each reached different conclusions based on two very different sets of facts.

In *Suisman, Shapiro, Wool, Brennan, Gray & Greenberg, P.C. v. Suisman, Shapiro and Suisman & Shapiro*, the federal district court in Connecticut dealt with the sons of the founding members of a well-known New London, Connecticut law firm that left the firm of their fathers to open their own law firm about 10 blocks away. They attempted to use their surnames in the same order as the two names used by the established firm started by each of their fathers.

By contrast, Indiana's high court addressed the use of the same name by two unrelated persons, one in Rushville, Indiana, and the other about 100 miles away in Fort Wayne, Indiana. In *Keaton and Keaton v. Keaton, Keaton d/b/a Keaton and Keaton*, the trial court and the Court of Appeals were upheld in determining that the firm in Fort Wayne was entitled to use their lawyers' surname and that the firm in Rushville did not meet its burden to demonstrate, in the context of a summary judgment motion, that the name Keaton had acquired a unique association with the firm in Rushville, nor was there sufficient evidence presented of confusion in order to establish infringement by the firm in Fort Wayne. The court also noted that there was no evidence that the firm in Rushville—however well established in its own town—had any name recognition in Fort Wayne, over 100 miles away.

Both cases discussed the "name issue" in the context of trade name infringement and the related concept of unfair competition. Though at common law there was a right to use one's name similar to the right to use other property, modern authority holds that surnames are only protectable if they acquire secondary meaning and come to be associated with a particular business through use. The Indiana case also discussed the tort of "passing off one's services for that of another" through the use of confusingly similar trade names with the net result of deceiving the public. However, unlike infringement, that tort requires intentional misrepresentation, which was not found by the court.

The federal court in Connecticut discussed the trademark infringement claim in much greater detail in addition to addressing several state statutes relating to unfair competition. The court found the name "Suisman Shapiro" had acquired a secondary meaning as a long-standing provider of legal services in New London, Connecticut, distinct from the individuals whose names appear in the name of the "first" firm to be called Suisman Shapiro in that city. The court concluded that there was a likelihood of confusion under the Lanham Act with regard to the marks, or names, used by the parties, and that summary judgment on that issue was appropriate. Based on that finding, the court also found support for a claim under Connecticut's common law of unfair competition as well as the state trademark statute and the state unfair trade practices act. The court permanently enjoined the new firm from using any combination of the names Suisman or Shapiro, in addition to enjoining them from advertising under the prohibited names or maintaining a telephone listing under those names.

There is no geographical limitation contained in the wording of the *Suisman* court's ruling. Thus by comparison with the *Keaton* case that we discussed earlier in this article, the reader will likely wonder if the result would have been the same if the newer firm had opened an office 100 miles away from the firm that their fathers founded. The *Suisman* court analyzes in great detail the cases that address the many factors applied in a determination of whether or not there is a likelihood of confusion by the consumer. In light of the proximity of the firms, and the many years of association among the members of both firms in the *Suisman* case, the *Keaton* case dealt with an almost diametrically opposite set of facts.

In sum, these cases are not establishing new law, but they provide useful reminders about the limitations on the ability to use one's own name for the establishment of one's own law firm. ◆

Francis G.X. Pileggi is the founding partner of the Wilmington, Delaware, office of Fox Rothschild LLP. He is co-chair of the Ethics Subcommittee of the Business and Commercial Litigation Committee of the ABA's Litigation Section. He maintains a blog at www.delawarelitigation.com. He often writes on issues of ethics, professionalism, business law and electronic discovery.

Advertisements Touting Designations as 'Super Lawyer' or 'Best Lawyer in America' Violate New Jersey Rules of Professional Conduct

Opinion 39 issued by the Committee on Attorney Advertising appointed by the New Jersey Supreme Court, on July 19, 2006 [185 N.J.L.J. 360], has determined that advertisements in any medium of distribution publicizing certain New Jersey attorneys as "Super Lawyers" or "Best Lawyers in America" violate the prohibition against advertisements that are comparative in nature, as proscribed under the New Jersey version of Rule 7.1(a)(3).

However, on August 18, 2006 the New Jersey Supreme Court stayed the enforcement of the opinion pending its further consideration of the matter. Nonetheless, a summary of the committee's conclusion merits discussion.

The committee concluded that the comparisons are also likely to create an unjustified expectation about results in violation of Rule 7.1(a)(2) of the New Jersey Rules of Professional Conduct. The committee was asked to address advertisements that appeared first in a 2005 *New Jersey Monthly* magazine and a subsequent stand-alone magazine both devoted primarily to advertisements by law firms promoting their designations as "Super Lawyers." A *New Jersey Monthly* "Super Lawyers" magazine and subsequent stand-alone addition were also published in 2006. The advertisements in question were primarily focused on congratulating the chosen lawyers for their designation as "Super Lawyers." The designation as "Super Lawyers" has led to increased marketing by attorneys in the form of advertisements in local publications, as well as brochures, telephone book listings and Web sites.

The committee also received inquiries concerning the propriety of advertising and promotion of a New Jersey attorney's status as a "Best Lawyer in America." The committee noted differences in the methodology of selection for those designations but reached the same conclusion that both designations, when advertised, violated the applicable New Jersey Rules of Professional Conduct.

In an interview for the *Wall Street Journal's Law Blog*, the chairman of the New Jersey Committee on Attorney Advertising said that although the committee could not prohibit the publisher from publishing such advertisements, the committee did have the power to penalize attorneys who participated in violation of the rules. Specifically, the chair of the committee was quoted on the *WSJ Law Blog* as warning that if the "Super Lawyers" edition is published next year and lawyers chose to advertise in it, "they will run afoul of the Rules of Professional Conduct and do so at their own peril."

See http://blogs.wsj.com/law/2006/07/21/new-jersey-says-super-lawyers-is-super-misleading/. The chair added that: "The state takes seriously its role of protecting the public from deceptive legal practices." *Id.*

The reasoning behind the decision of the committee was based on the proscription in Rule 7.1(a)(3), which states that a communication is misleading if it "compares the lawyer's service with other lawyers' services." The inherently comparative superlative designation is not within the approved ambit of the New Jersey rules because they are based on an assessment by the attorney or other members of the bar, or devised by persons or organizations outside the bar, that lack both court approval and objective verification of the ability of the lawyer. The committee further reasoned that the "self-aggrandizing titles have the potential to lead an unwary consumer to believe that the lawyers so described are, by virtue of this manufactured title, superior to their colleagues that practice in the same areas of law." Moreover, the advertisements violate Rule 7.1(a)(2), which provides that a communication is misleading if it "is likely to create an unjustified expectation about results the lawyer can achieve…." The committee reasoned that when a potential client reads such advertising and considers hiring a "super" attorney, the superlative designation induces the client to feel that the results that can be achieved by this attorney are likely to surpass those that can be achieved by a mere "ordinary" attorney. The committee concluded that "this simplistic use of a media-generated sound bite title clearly has the capacity to materially mislead the public." The Committee also described in detail the problems with the advertisements or "text that appears along with the designations as an article but may be paid for in a manner similar to an advertisement."

An August 1, 2006 article on *Law.com* quoted from an e-mail by the publisher sent to all the 1,669 New Jersey attorneys in the Super Lawyers survey, which said: "…we disagree with **every aspect** of the Committee's opinion and intend to challenge it with every means at our disposal." (emphasis added). According to the *Law.com* article, the New Jersey opinion is unique.

A cursory review of the *ABA/BNA Lawyers' Manual on Professional Conduct* did not reveal any similar opinions from any other states. If anyone is aware of any similar opinions or rulings in other states, I would appreciate you bringing that to my attention. Thank you. ◆

Francis G.X. Pileggi is the founding partner of the Wilmington, Delaware office of Fox Rothschild LLP, an AmLaw 200 member. He maintains a blog at www.delaware-litigation.com which summarizes Delaware business litigation cases and also highlights topics on ethics and e-discovery. His e-mail address is fpileggi@foxrothschild.com.

Unsolicited E-Mails Not Subject to Rules Applicable to Client Communications

*T*he San Diego County Bar Association, through its Legal Ethics Committee, issued Ethics Opinion 2006-1 recently to address the issue of how to treat the receipt of unsolicited e-mails containing confidential information.

In particular, the Opinion addressed the situation where a lawyer received an unsolicited e-mail from a potential client who was a driver in a multi-car accident, after the lawyer had already been retained by a separate driver in the same multi-car pileup. The unsolicited e-mail contained confidential information that was potentially harmful to the sender of the unsolicited e-mail, but it was helpful to the previous client that had already been retained by the same lawyer.

The Legal Ethics Committee concluded as follows: (1) The unsolicited e-mail was not deemed confidential for purposes of the applicable rules. Private information from a non-client sent in an unsolicited e-mail is not required to be held in confidence if the lawyer did not have an opportunity to warn or stop the non-client before the communication was delivered; (2) The attorney involved in this case was not precluded from representing the prior client, and the lawyer was entitled to use the subsequent information received in the unsolicited e-mail.

The policy basis for the opinion of the Committee was three-fold. First, the Committee encourages the widest possible access to legal services. Second, public policy must support the confidentiality of communications by those seeking legal services once both parties determine that a client relationship is appropriate. Third, public policy should protect current clients from conflicts created by unsolicited confidential information sent from prospective clients.

Citing California law, the Committee described the basis of a lawyer's duty of confidentiality and communications protected by the attorney/client privilege. The Committee noted that the triggering of an attorney/client privilege does not always require the actual retention of an attorney. The reasoning for this is to protect the information of clients whose retention was declined by the attorney. Once the privilege attaches, moreover, the attorney has a duty to refuse to disclose confidential information.

In order for the duty of confidentiality to apply, however, two prerequisites must be satisfied under California law according to the Opinion: (1) The party must be considered by the lawyer as a possible "client"; and (2) The communication between the person and the attorney must be "confidential." Under Section 951 of the California Evidence Code, a "client" is defined as a person who consults a lawyer for the purpose of securing legal advice. Thus, the first requirement is that the client must "consult" a lawyer. Also, the purpose of the consultation must be to secure legal advice. Moreover, the attorney must be solicited for the legal services in his or her professional capacity as a lawyer (citing Restatement (3rd) of the Law Governing Lawyers, Section 70(c)).

The Committee cited to a California Supreme Court decision in People v. Gionis, 9 Cal. 4th 1196, 1202-1205 (1995), in connection with the requirement that the attorney have an opportunity to prevent a prospective client from engaging in a consultation which would invoke the duties of confidentiality. That case was cited for the rule that the privilege does not extend to disclosures made after an attorney refuses to accept representation, because in that context the person could have no reasonable expectation of being represented by an attorney after such a rejection was made. See also Opinion No. 2003-161 of the Standing Committee on Professional Responsibility and Conduct of the State Bar of California.

Francis G.X. Pileggi, Esquire is the founding partner of the Wilmington, Delaware office of Fox Rothschild LLP, a member of the AmLaw 200. He maintains a blog at www.delawarelitigation.com, which summarizes key Chancery Court decisions as well as related business litigation cases and commentary. He is co-chair of the Ethics Subcommittee of the Business and Commercial Litigation Committee of the ABA's Litigation Section. His e-mail address is: fpileggi@foxrothschild.com. Suggestions for topics of future ethics columns are encouraged.

The Committee concluded that because the attorney did not have an opportunity to expressly refuse to represent the person who sent the unsolicited e-mail, it would be unreasonable for the sender of the e-mail to believe that her unsolicited message would be confidentially treated.

The Committee determined that as long as the attorney notifies the sender of an e-mail as soon as "reasonably possible after it has become apparent that the sender wants to consult with the attorney" and unequivocally explains to the sender that the attorney cannot represent the sender, that attorney does not acquire duties of confidentiality in connection with the review by the attorney of an unsolicited e-mail from an unknown sender.

The Committee noted that substantially similar results have been expressed by the Arizona State Bar Ethics Committee in its Opinion 02-04, as well as in Formal Opinion 2001-1 of the Association of the Bar of the City of New York, and that similar reasoning was employed in Comment 2 to Rule 1.18

of the American Bar Association's Model Rules of Professional Conduct.

The San Diego County Bar Association Legal Ethics Committee further reasoned that if the "mere sending of an unsolicited e-mail seeking legal services to an attorney" would trigger a duty of confidentiality, it would create an unmanageable risk for attorneys. They added that: "Such a rule would give unilateral and unfettered control to non-lawyer senders of e-mail... Not only does this create the risk of non-lawyer abuse and "tactical tricks" but also gives the innocent prospective consumer of legal services a means of disrupting existing attorney/client relationships by creating conflicts of interest."

In sum, this is a thoughtful opinion that strikes a reasonable balance between the important duties of confidentiality and the modern reality that allows unsolicited e-mails to be sent with ease. It appears that the best practice would be to reply to any sender of e-mails seeking legal representation to clarify that no such attorney/client relationship or duty of confidentiality has been established.◆

Recent Court Decisions Enforce Minimum Standards of Attorney Behavior

ETHICS COLUMN: Francis G.X. Pileggi

Several recent decisions from around the country indicate that some courts do take seriously the need to enforce minimum standards of attorney behavior. In this short column, I highlight briefly only two of those recent court opinions. The issues addressed are not matters of competence, but rather deal with the behavior of lawyers towards others, regardless of the substantive ability of the lawyer.

For example, the Delaware Supreme Court recently found violations of Rule 3.5(d) and Rule 8.4(d) of the Delaware Lawyers' Rules of Professional Conduct in connection with statements that were made in an opening brief and a reply brief filed in the Delaware Superior Court. Rule 3.5(d) provides that a lawyer shall not engage in conduct intended to disrupt a tribunal or engage in undignified or discourteous conduct that is degrading to a tribunal. Rule 8.4(d) provides that it is professional misconduct for a lawyer to engage in conduct that is prejudicial to the administration of justice.

The court found that the conduct went beyond "merely" unprofessional and that the rules were violated because the pleadings filed with the court contained "unnecessary invective and rhetoric and were obnoxious [as well as] unnecessarily sarcastic and strident in tone." The court noted that the duty to the tribunal takes precedence over the interests of a client because officers of the court are obligated to represent clients within the bounds of the Rules of Ethics. The opinion quotes former U.S. Supreme Court Justice Sandra Day O'Connor where she stated that "incivility disserves the client because it wastes time and energy - - time that is billed to the client at hundreds of dollars an hour, and energy that is better spent working on the case than working over the opponent." The Delaware Supreme Court also cited one of its prior opinions of 15 years ago when it stated: "simply put, insulting conduct toward opposing counsel, and disparaging a court's integrity are unacceptable by any standard."

The court further reasoned that: "zealous advocacy never requires disruptive, disrespectful, degrading or disparaging rhetoric. The use of such rhetoric crosses the line from acceptable forceful advocacy into unethical conduct that violates the Delaware Lawyers' Rules of Professional Conduct."

Thus, the Delaware Supreme Court is now on record as ruling that disrespectful, degrading or disparaging rhetoric violates the ethical rules that apply to lawyers. What is not entirely clear because it was not addressed by the court, is whether disrespectful, disparaging or degrading behavior by one lawyer to another, in face to face meetings or in written and oral exchanges outside of court, would also be considered unethical conduct. Although also beyond the scope of the opinion, I mention as an aside, the truism incorporated in the rules that a lawyers' staff are not permitted to violate the standards that the lawyers themselves are required to uphold. See *In Re Abbott*, (Del. Supr., May 2, 2007).

In *Redwood v. Dobson*, (7th Cir., Feb. 7, 2007), lawyers' behavior during depositions was analyzed. It is not always easy to draw the line between what has become part of the "rough and tumble" of a deposition, as opposed to abusive behavior that rises to the level justifying an attorney walking out of the deposition. Judge Frank Easterbrook of the U.S. Court of Appeals for the Seventh Circuit has now added to the case law that helps litigators answer that question. The Court in Redwood severely criticized not only the lawyer taking the deposition, but also the lawyer defending it for, inter alia, not stopping the deposition to file a motion for protective order - - instead of instructing the deponent not to answer a question which was clearly meant only to harass and annoy but which was not within the limited scope of questions the rule allows an attorney to instruct the deponent not to answer.

Though not condoning boorish behavior, Carolyn Elefant wrote respectfully in a recent law.com article available at the following link, http://legalblogwatch. typepad.com/legal_blog_watch/2007/05/lawyer_ behaving.html#comments, that the panel deciding the *Redwood* case, while undoubtedly smart, fair and exemplary jurists, did not appear to give any consideration to the practical rough and tumble schoolyard-like realities of some depositions, and the increased (and perhaps prohibitive) cost if a deposition were stopped in order to file a motion to compel, or the havoc wreaked on scheduling deadlines if the deponent and his counsel walked out so as to file a motion for a protective order, under Rule 30(d), every time a lawyer taking or defending a deposition violated the rules (along with the uncertainty of when the motion would be heard and how long it would be before the deposition were rescheduled--as it is not always possible to get a judge on the phone during the deposition.) For Delaware cases on point regarding deposition practice, see the Delaware Supreme Court's famous decision in *Paramount Communications, Inc. v. QVC Network, Inc.,* 637 A.2d 34, n.28 (Del. 1994) (condemning *ad hominem* attacks by counsel), and also a Delaware Superior Court decision in *State v. Mumford,* 731 A.2d 831, 835 (Del. Super. 1999) (revoking pro hac vice status because of abusive deposition behavior).

Steven Lubet, writing in *The American Lawyer,* on May 1, 2007, suggests that the *Redwood* decision may embolden bullies to pursue improper lines of inquiry in a deposition, knowing that their opponents will either need to answer every question, no matter how obnoxious, or adjourn the deposition, thus incurring the added cost and delay of filing a motion with the court. This approach may engender a new game of chicken, which may inure to the benefit of the more well-heeled party who can more easily afford the cost and delay of not finishing the deposition in the most efficient manner.

The almost-Hobson's choice presented by this situation is made more difficult based on my experience that even after a judge addresses the issue created by the unruly opposing counsel, there is no certainty that the time and effort spent to bring the issue before the court will be worth the extra time and cost (which is never fully reimbursed).

Francis G.X. Pileggi, Esquire is the founding partner of the Wilmington, Delaware office of Fox Rothschild LLP, a member of the AmLaw 200. He maintains a blog at www.delawarelitigation.com, which summarizes key Delaware Chancery Court and Supreme Court decisions as well as related business litigation cases and commentary. He is co-chair of the Ethics Subcommittee of the Business and Commercial Litigation Committee of the ABA's Litigation Section. His e-mail address is: fpileggi@foxrothschild.com. Suggestions for topics of future ethics columns are encouraged.

My partner, Sheldon K. Rennie, deserves public praise for his comments on a draft of this article. ✴

Two Recent Court Decisions Address Important Conflict of Interest Issues

ETHICS COLUMN: FRANCIS G.X. PILEGGI

Two recent court decisions remind us of the serious problems that can be caused by not carefully examining the issues raised by a potential conflict of interest. In *Board of Managers of Eleventh Street Loftominium Association v. Wabash Loftominium LLC*, 2007 WL 2416817 (Ill. App. 1 Dist.) ("Wabash"), the Illinois Court of Appeals disqualified a law firm for not complying with Rule of Professional Conduct 1.7 relating to conflicts with current clients. In *Attorney Grievance Commission of Maryland v. Siskind*, 2007 WL 2404800 (Md.), the Court of Appeals of Maryland applied Rule 1.9 to address conflicts with a former client.

In *Wabash*, the Illinois Appellate Court determined that the law firm involved did not disclose the conflict and did not obtain the necessary consent in connection with claims against an affiliate of a company that the firm had represented for several years. The court reasoned that the management group of the firm's existing client, as well as the individual defendants and the corporate defendants in the litigation at issue, were substantially similar. The court was not persuaded by the argument for purposes of this disqualification analysis that the separate corporations should be treated as distinct entities for conflict purposes. The court distinguished Illinois Ethics Opinion 95-15 (1996) which generally permits a lawyer to represent one corporate defendant who is adverse to a corporate affiliate of that client. The court noted that Op. 95-15 provides for several exceptions to that general rule, including "where the client corporation and the subsidiary in question have the same management group." That exception to the general rule applied here because the court found that the management group for all the entities involved consisted of substantially the same individuals.

The court also addressed ABA Formal Ethics Op. 95-390 (1995) which addressed conflicts in the corporate family context. Op. 95-390 stated that an analysis under Rule 1.7 acknowledged the importance of factual circumstances and emphasized that "the fact that a lawyer for a subsidiary was engaged by and reports to an officer or general counsel for its parent may support the inference that the corporate parent reasonably expects to be treated as a client." In this case, the attorney involved was engaged by and reported to the management group that ran the parent corporation, as well as the subsidiary and affiliated corporations, which would lead that management group to believe that they were included within the family of existing clients of the law firm. The court was critical of the fact that the attorney took no affirmative action to inform the management group that it was ending their long-term attorney-client relationship. The law firm attempted to argue that its representation and relationship had ended but the court relied on the fact that there were 60 matters opened over the last 7 years for which 15 members of the firm billed over $175,000 in fees. Thus, the court rejected the applicability of any analysis under Rule 1.9, which applies to former clients. Nor was the court impressed with the screening of any attorneys who had done work for the affiliated entities. The court reasoned that "there is no provision in Rule 1.7 for an internal screening memorandum... to take the place of affirmative disclosure and informed consent."

Of particular educational value was the discussion by Justice McBride about why the attorney-client relationship was not considered by the court to have been ended properly for purposes of a conflict analysis. The court, in rejecting the law firm's argument that its relationship with its client was over, stated that "the subject law firm's relationship with its client was sufficiently continuous, and the mere fortuity that the client did not require more extensive or frequent services than he did cannot be the escape hatch the law firm would have it be." See *Manoir-Electroalloys Corp. v. Amalloy Corp.*, 711 F.Supp. 188, 194 (D.N.J. 1989). The court distinguished other cases that dealt with clearly circumscribed and specific tasks as opposed to a broader and more general type of representation of an entity.

In support of its finding of a Rule 1.7 conflict, the court cited to *International Business Machines v. Levin*, 579 F.2d 271, 281 (3d Cir. 1978), for the position that merely because no specific assignment from the client was pending; a continuous client relationship can be found based on a past pattern of repeated engagements, even if on a fee for service basis, as opposed to a standing retainer agreement. *Compare generally, Elonix I.P. Holdings, Ltd. v. Apple Computer, Inc.*, 142 F.Supp.2d 579 (D.Del. 2001) (separate offices of same large law firm representing and suing international corporation in unrelated matters, would <u>not</u> be disqualified on conflict of interest basis).

11

In the *Siskind* case, the court addressed a messy set of facts involving the minefield that is known as the representation of joint clients who subsequently have a disagreement. The troubles of this attorney began when he agreed to represent only one of the two clients that he formally represented jointly, in a suit where that one client sued the lawyer's former client. The court found that the rule on former client conflicts—Rule 1.9—was violated after the attorney filed suit on behalf of one of the joint clients against the other in connection with matters related to the lawyer's former representation of both of them.

The attorney began the joint representation when he formed an entity that his two clients obtained a 50% interest in. After one of the partners bought out the interest of the other partner in the entity, the attorney filed suit for breach of contract against both the entity that he formed and the one partner who had purchased the entire entity. Maryland's high court found that the attorney did not obtain the consent of the former client to represent an existing client in a substantially related matter in which the current client's interests were materially adverse to those of the former client, in violation of Rule 1.9. By operation of law, the court explained that the attorney was presumed to possess confidential information relating to the entity that he formed and the former client.

The court rejected the argument that the "joint representation doctrine" or "common interest doctrine" required a different result. An important distinction was made between the attorney-client privilege and the ethical duty to preserve a client's confidences. The court underscored that the ethical duty to preserve a client's confidences is broader than the evidentiary privilege, encompassing not only confidential information, but all knowledge acquired by the client.

The court also referred to the Comment to MRPC 1.9 which provides: "The underlying question is whether the lawyer was so involved in the matter that the subsequent representation can be justly regarded as a changing of sides in that matter in question." *See St. Albans Fin. Co. v. Blair*, 559 F.Supp. 523, 526, *aff'd*, 725 F.2d 670 (3d. Cir. 1983). The court explained its result as follows: "This type of fair-weather loyalty and former client poaching is forbidden; an attorney may not abandon the duty not to harm a former client when circumstances make it expedient and/or self-serving to do so."✷

Francis G.X. Pileggi, Esq. is the founding partner of the Wilmington, Delaware office of Fox Rothschild LLP, a member of the AmLaw 200. He maintains a blog at www.delawarelitigation.com, which summarizes key Delaware Chancery Court and Supreme Court decisions as well as related business litigation cases and commentary. He is on the Editorial Board of "The Bencher" and the ABA's Litigation Ethics publication. His e-mail address is: fpileggi@foxrothschild.com. Suggestions for topics of future ethics columns are encouraged.

Class Member Not Entitled To Full Panoply Of Attorney/Client Relationship Benefits

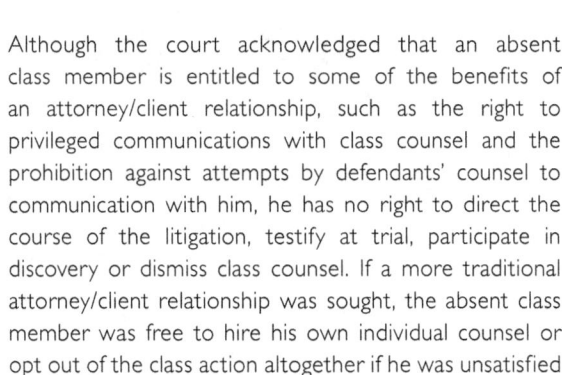

A recent decision from the Appellate Division of the New York Supreme Court held that an absent class member is not entitled to the files of co-lead counsel accumulated during the course of two consolidated federal class actions, nor was the absent class member entitled to attorney work product. *Wyly v. Milberg Weiss Bershad and Schulman, LLP*, 2007 WL 4533380 (NY Supr., App. Div., Dec. 27, 2007). After the securities class actions were dismissed, and the court approved a settlement and an award of attorneys' fees, a class member attempted to have the settlement rescinded based on allegations of fraud by an officer of the defendant company with whom the settlement was reached. The attempt to "relieve" the settlement class from the final judgment approving the settlement was filed under Rule 60(b) of the Federal Rules of Civil Procedure. In the course of the motion to have the settlement opened, the absent class member also sought the discovery materials that lead counsel had obtained. The absent class member also sought e-mails, attorney notes, internal memoranda, privilege logs and all research related to the representation of the class members in the class actions.

The Appellate Division reversed the lower court and rejected the argument that an absent class member was entitled to the same range of rights and privileges that a traditional client was entitled to—especially after the case was nominally closed. Thus, the court refused to follow the decision relied on by the lower court which provided that in a traditional attorney/client relationship, the client was entitled to full access, with narrow exceptions, to all the documents in an attorney's file, including work product material, absent a claim for unpaid legal fees. *See generally, Matter of Sage Realty Corp. v. Proskauer Rose Goetz and Mendelsohn*, 91 NY2d 30 (1997).

The *Wyly* court, however, recognized an observation made by courts and commentators alike, that the relationship between appointed counsel and an absent member in a class action differs substantially from that found in a traditional attorney/client relationship. *See, e.g., In Re: J.P. Morgan Chase Cash Balance Litig.*, 242 F.R.D. 265, 277 (2007); *Phillips Petroleum Co. v. Shutts*, 472 U.S. 797, 810 – 811 (1985).

Although the court acknowledged that an absent class member is entitled to some of the benefits of an attorney/client relationship, such as the right to privileged communications with class counsel and the prohibition against attempts by defendants' counsel to communication with him, he has no right to direct the course of the litigation, testify at trial, participate in discovery or dismiss class counsel. If a more traditional attorney/client relationship was sought, the absent class member was free to hire his own individual counsel or opt out of the class action altogether if he was unsatisfied with his limited role.

In order to avoid the unduly burdensome potential, even after the end of litigation, that would result from a multitude of requests from absent class members for counsel's entire file, the court adopted a requirement that absent class members establish their entitlement to class counsel's file on a case-by-case basis. *See generally, In Re: Intel Corp. Microprocessor Anti-Trust Litigation*, 2007 WL 4323007 (D.Del., Dec. 6, 2007) (court determined that defendant was not entitled to discovery relating to a class representatives' financial information in light of that data being irrelevant to class certification issues particularly where counsel was contractually obligated to advance litigation costs); *Ginsburg v. Philadelphia Stock Exchange*, 2007 WL 2982238 (Del. Ch., Oct. 9, 2007) (Chancery Court allowed limited discovery by an objector to a proposed settlement of a class action, and permitted access to discovery already taken, subject to a confidentiality order, so that the objector would be in a position to assess the fairness of and the detailed basis for the settlement). *

*Francis G.X. Pileggi is the founding partner of the Wilmington, Delaware office of Fox Rothschild LLP, an AmLaw 200 firm. His blog at www.delawarelitigation.com summarizes all the key decisions on corporate and commercial law from the Delaware Court of Chancery and Delaware Supreme Court. His e-mail address is: fpileggi@foxrothschild.com.

ETHICS COLUMN: FRANCIS G.X. PILEGGI

Texas Court Rejects Claims against Law Firm for Exceeding Litigation Budget and Raising Fees

This is a short summary of a decision by the Court of Appeals for Fifth District of Texas that rejected claims brought against a law firm based on allegations that the firm breached its fiduciary duties to a client for failing to keep its fees within an estimated litigation budget and also for raising fees during the representation without giving written notice to the client. In McGuire, Craddock, Strother & Hale, P.C. v. TransContinental Realty Investors, Inc., et al., No. 05-07-00050-CV (April 8, 2008), the appellate court reviewed a jury verdict in favor of the law firm in its lawsuit to collect attorneys' fees that the trial judge had set aside notwithstanding the verdict.

The background facts involved a group of office buildings in Dallas that suffered water and fire damage. The law firm represented the managers of the office buildings in claims against their insurer which resulted in a $17.1 million payment from the insurer.

After the litigation began against the insurance company, the client also requested that claims be pursued against the parties responsible for the losses at the office buildings. The law firm agreed to the additional representation on the same fee terms as were agreed to in the litigation against the insurance company. Approximately a year after the representation began, the realty company hired a new assistant general counsel who was responsible for monitoring all of its outside litigation. At a meeting in September 1997, that person requested the law firm to prepare a litigation budget, which estimated fees between $530,000 to $650,000 to complete the litigation through trial. At some point during the year 1999, the "second" litigation against third-parties intensified and became very contentious. During a pre-mediation meeting in December 1999, the new assistant general counsel allegedly first became aware that the fees were approaching $1.25 million (although monthly bills were sent). In April of 2000, after trying unsuccessfully to work out a payment plan for the fees that exceeded the budgeted amount, the client terminated the law firm.

The law firm sued for its attorneys' fees, alleging claims for breach of the fee agreement and fraudulent inducement. The client counterclaimed for breach of contract, fraud, breach of fiduciary duty, negligence and negligent misrepresentation. The jury found in favor of the law firm on both its breach of contract and fraudulent inducement claims, and against the client on their counterclaims. The trial judge, however, granted a judgment notwithstanding the verdict and the parties appealed.

On appeal, the law firm argued that the verdict in its favor was supported by legally sufficient evidence that the law firm complied with its fiduciary duty and the appellate court agreed. The appellate court noted that the essence of a claim for breach of fiduciary duty focuses on whether an attorney obtained an improper benefit from representing the client and whether he breached that duty by subordinating his client's interests to his own.

Among the primary arguments of the client on appeal were that the law firm did not advise the client in writing when it raised hourly rates and that the law firm failed to manage the underlying litigation within the proposed litigation budget or update the proposed budget.

The appellate court observed that the written engagement letter for the initial lawsuit against the insurance company was fully complied with by the law firm when they submitted monthly bills and the client paid them without complaint. The bills did not list the hourly rates of the attorneys and included some block-billing but did describe the service performed and the name of the person performing the service, as well as the number of hours billed for the service. When the second litigation was requested, the parties orally agreed to continue to bill as they had in the initial matter and those payments were also submitted and paid in the same format on a monthly basis without complaint until October of 1999 when the client stopped paying.

Justice Carolyn Wright, writing for the Court of Appeals, noted that even if the Texas Rules of Professional Conduct support the argument that an increase in the hourly rate should have been more clearly brought to the attention of the client, those rules do not define standards of civil liability for lawyers, nor does the violation of these rules give rise to a private cause of action. Moreover, any such violation does not create a presumption that a legal duty to a client has been breached. Moreover, Justice Wright emphasized that the evidence at trial demonstrated that the law firm did make the client aware that it periodically increased its rates.

Regarding the litigation budget allegedly being exceeded, the court found evidence in the record that the law firm emphasized in writing when it submitted the litigation budget that there was an inherent difficulty in forecasting "legal expenses with any degree of accuracy, and it is quite possible that legal fees could be substantially more or less than this estimate." Moreover, the law firm emphasized in writing that the "budget projection does not represent any form of guarantee or assurance of a maximum fee or that the legal fees will not exceed the projected amounts, nor does it represent a guarantee or assurance of any particular outcome."

ETHICS COLUMN: FRANCIS G.X. PILEGGI

In sum, the appellate court concluded that the trial court erred in granting judgment notwithstanding the verdict because there was sufficient evidence to support the finding of the jury that the law firm did not breach any fiduciary duty owed to its client. Among the many observations that could be made about this case is that the dynamics of the client relationship seem to have changed in the middle of the representation when a new assistant general counsel was hired and assumed the responsibility for overseeing the litigation. It is not uncommon when representing companies that the client's "contact person" may change after litigation has been authorized and it is not always true that the new person responsible for the client relationship is as enthusiastic about the litigation as the original person who authorized it.

It is well settled that courts have supervisory power to determine the reasonableness of fees. See generally, In Re Savell, 876 So. 2d 308, 19 Law. Man. Prof. Conduct 200 (Miss. 2004). See also Alaska Electrical Pension Fund v. Brown, 941 A.2d 1011 (Del. 2007) (reviewing attorneys' fees in class action settlements). Of historical interest is that one author has traced the custom of hourly billing by attorneys to a study in the 1960s that those who recorded their time on a daily basis generated more revenue than those who did not. See Shepherd, Discovery Leads to Hourly Billing, 1999 U .Ill. L. Rev. 91 (1999). Cf. Restatement of the Law Governing Lawyers, Section 34 (2000) (overarching guideline for attorneys' fees is reasonableness).

I suppose one lesson from this case is to make sure that any new contact person at a client's company who becomes responsible for overseeing litigation midway through a lawsuit is updated on the original terms of the engagement agreed to by his predecessor, although in the end there is no certain way to avoid client claims.

Francis G.X. Pileggi is the founding partner of the Wilmington, Delaware, office of Fox Rothschild LLP, an AmLaw 200 firm. His blog at www.delawarelitigation.com summarizes all the key decisions on corporate and commercial law from the Delaware Court of Chancery and Delaware Supreme Court, and includes posts on legal ethics. His e-mail address is: fpileggi@foxrothschild.com.

ETHICS COLUMN: FRANCIS G.X. PILEGGI

New York Court Upholds Arbitration Clause in Fee Agreement with Client

The Supreme Court of the State of New York issued a decision recently upholding an arbitration clause in a fee agreement with a client. This is a short summary of that opinion. In *Connectu, Inc. v. Quinn Emanuel Urquhart Oliver & Hedges, LLP*, N.Y. Supr. Ct., No. 602082/08 (Sept. 12, 2008), the Court ruled that the arbitration provision was neither contrary to public policy nor was it infirm for any other reasons that would otherwise bar the enforceability of the arbitration clause in the fee agreement.

Background

The background of the case involved the group of individuals who had sued Facebook, Inc. concerning the ownership of the social networking Web site, Facebook.com. The plaintiffs in this case were that same group that were formerly Quinn Emanuel clients. They had initially been represented by a nationally-known law firm who had been handling the litigation for several years. In September 2007, the plaintiffs engaged Quinn Emanuel, and after lengthy discussions they entered into a contingency fee agreement. That contingency fee agreement was reviewed by separate independent counsel for the plaintiffs, and eventually the terms were agreed upon and the engagement letter was executed.

The arbitration clause in the engagement letter required binding arbitration with the American Arbitration Association in the event of any disputes between Quinn Emanuel and the plaintiffs. After Quinn Emanuel represented them in the Facebook litigation for several months, settlement was achieved in February of 2008 through mediation.

The plaintiffs did not pay the attorneys' fees that Quinn Emanuel claimed to be owed, however. Instead they terminated Quinn Emanuel's representation and hired new counsel, without success, to attack the settlement. Quinn Emanuel initiated arbitration proceedings claiming $13 million plus expenses pursuant to its September 2007 fee agreement. Although the arbitration demand was filed with the AAA in April 2008; because a separate action was commenced, unsuccessfully attempting to challenge the settlement agreement, Quinn Emanuel asked the AAA to hold the arbitration in abeyance until that separate action was completed. In June 2008 when the Facebook settlement was upheld in that separate action by a federal court as enforceable, Quinn Emanuel then instructed the AAA to reinstate the arbitration proceedings to collect its fee.

Legal Arguments

The former clients presented a long list of arguments to support their position that the Quinn Emanuel claims were not subject to arbitration. For example they argued that the arbitration clause was obtained without their consent and that the arbitration clause violated the public policy of the State of New York because it was obtained in breach of Quinn Emanuel's duties to its clients and applicable rules of legal ethics. They also argued that Quinn Emanuel waived its rights to arbitration. In sum, the Court rejected all of these arguments.

The former clients relied on a rule in New York that provides for arbitration of fee disputes between attorneys and clients. However, the arbitration provisions of that New York State rule do not apply to fee disputes in excess of $50,000, as here.

The New York Court relied on basic contract principles in its reasoning that the written agreement involved was complete, clear and unambiguous and must be enforced according to the plain meaning of its terms. There was no showing, the Court found, that the arbitration clause was obtained without consent or that it was the result of fraud, misrepresentation or duress.

Neither the argument that the fee agreement was infirm due to a provision that it shortened the statute of limitations for claims arising out of the engagement to one year, nor the provision that a 1.5% per month late fee for legal fees owed beyond sixty days, was sufficient to establish any grounds for not enforcing the arbitration clause. The Court also made short work of the argument that Quinn Emanuel waived its right to arbitrate.

Of course, this decision is not binding on other states but it should give hope to lawyers who want to provide for the benefits that in some cases can be enjoyed by the arbitration of disputes with clients, as opposed to litigation, to the extent that litigation through the court system in some instances takes longer and may be more of a public exercise. See generally Rule 1.5 of the Model Rules of Professional Conduct, comment 9 (encouraging arbitration or mediation of fee disputes); ABA/BNA Lawyers' Manual on Professional Conduct, Section 41:101 (2008) (citing states that have upheld mandatory arbitration programs or arbitration clauses in fee agreements, that include California, Colorado, Georgia, Maine, New Jersey, Ohio and Pennsylvania). ✳

Francis G.X. Pileggi is the founding partner of the Wilmington, Delaware, office of Fox Rothschild LLP, an AmLaw 200 firm. His blog at www.delawarelitigation.com summarizes all the key decisions on corporate and commercial law from the Delaware Court of Chancery and Delaware Supreme Court, and includes posts on legal ethics. His e-mail address is fpileggi@foxrothschild.com.

Ethics Column
BY FRANCIS G.X. PILEGGI

Ethics: Counsel For Corporation Need Not Disclose Privileged Documents To Director Suing Corporation

An appellate court in California recently provided guidance to lawyers who are requested to give privileged documents to a director of a corporation when the attorney represents that corporation, whom that director is suing, in light of the attorney/client privilege. In *Triteck Telecom Ins. v. Superior Court*, 2009 Cal. App. LEXIS 7 (Jan. 7, 2009), the Court of Appeals of California addressed a situation where one of the corporation's directors filed suit to enforce his inspection rights as a director *after* he had already filed an action in his capacity as a shareholder against the corporation to vindicate his separate personal rights as a shareholder.

The California court held that, despite the generally broad right of a director to inspect books and records of a corporation, including documents protected by the attorney-client privilege, a "corporate director does not have the right to access documents covered by the attorney-client privilege that were generated in defense of a suit for damages that the director filed against the corporation" in his capacity as a shareholder.

BACKGROUND

Tritek Telecom, Inc. is a California corporation with two equal shareholders. Tritek originally had three directors. The Appollo Law Firm was hired by Tritek in connection with the resignation of one of the three directors.

Chik-Lun Mak was one of the two remaining directors and he also, through his controlled entity, was one of the two shareholders.

Mak initially sued the other remaining director and the corporation, Tritek, seeking (in his capacity as a shareholder) among other things a return of his $410,000 investment in Tritek, and the appointment of a provisional director. Thereafter, in his capacity as a director of Tritek, the instant suit by Mak was filed again against Tritek and the remaining director, seeking "to enforce his right as a director of Tritek to inspect Tritek's books and records."

LEGAL ANALYSIS

The Court of Appeals of California recited the basic privilege of a client to "refuse to disclose, and to prevent another from disclosing, a confidential communication between the client and his or her lawyer." The burden is on the party challenging the privilege to demonstrate that the privilege does not apply or that an exception or waiver applies.

Acknowledged at the outset was a director's fiduciary duty to act in the best interests of a corporation and its shareholders, in addition to the general right of a director to be given access to the corporation's books and records. The court balanced these competing rights and duties by observing first that Mak could not obtain via discovery in his shareholder action the documents that he was seeking in his separate lawsuit as a director. Moreover, the court emphasized that the filing of the shareholder action by Mak makes him an adversary to Tritek and that he "cannot take off his 'shareholder hat and swap it for his director's hat' and claim an absolute right to access all corporate documents. In this situation, a court may properly limit a director's inspection rights because the director's loyalties are divided and documents obtained by a director in his or her capacity as a director could be used to advance the director's personal interest in obtaining damages against the corporation." (citations omitted.)

Thus, the court concluded that "a corporate director does not have the right to access documents that are covered by the attorney-client privilege and were generated in defense of a suit for damages that the director filed against the corporation." *Id.* at *10. *See generally* Section 220 of the Delaware General Corporation Law (providing for limitations on the otherwise broad scope of documents to which a director is entitled) and *Schoon v. Smith*, 953 A.2d 196 (Del. 2008) (Delaware Supreme Court decision which held that directors cannot sue a corporation derivatively). *Compare Ryan v. Gifford*, 935 A.2d 258 (Del. Ch., 2007) (Delaware Chancery Court decision ordering production of a report that a company's lawyers provided to a special committee of the board, finding that the privilege was waived when a copy was sent to the whole board, some of whose members were the subject of the derivative suit involved in the report.)✳

Francis G.X. Pileggi is the founding partner of the Wilmington, Delaware, office of Fox Rothschild LLP, an AmLaw 200 firm. His blog, www.delawarelitigation.com, summarizes all the key decisions on corporate and commercial law from the Delaware Court of Chancery and Delaware Supreme Court, and includes posts on legal ethics. His e-mail address is: fpileggi@foxrothschild.com.

Ninth Circuit Finds Conflict of Interest in Incentive Provisions in Fee Agreements of Class Action Counsel

[Editor's Note: This column was co-authored by Francis G.X. Pileggi, Esquire and Sheldon K. Rennie, Esquire]

The U.S. Court of Appeals for the Ninth Circuit, in an opinion that has far reaching implications for class action counsel, found inherent conflicts of interests in a class action fee agreement that included incentive agreements that obligated class counsel to seek incentive awards for certain class representatives that would receive payments tied to the amount of the ultimate recovery. The opinion is published as *Rodriguez v. West Publishing Corp.*, No. 07-56643 (9th Cir. April 23, 2009). *See generally, Incentive Provisions in Retainer Contracts Created Conflicts in Class Action Litigation*, 25 Law. Man. Prof. Conduct 239 (May 13, 2009).

Notably, the Court of Appeals did not reverse the district court's finding that the class action settlement as a whole was fair and that the class was adequately represented, in part, because there were two other class representatives that had no incentive agreements and whose separate counsel was not conflicted.

The Settlement
The settlement arose out of an antitrust class action filed by several plaintiffs against West Publishing Corp., ("West") its subsidiary BAR/BRI, and Kaplan, Inc. ("Kaplan"). Plaintiffs asserted claims for antitrust violations pursuant to the Clayton Act and the Sherman Act. After the filing of the action, the parties engaged in lengthy settlement negotiations and eventually reached a settlement whereby West and Kaplan agreed to pay $49 million into a settlement fund.

Uniquely Structured Incentive Agreements
Prior to the filing of the class action and as part of their retention and fee agreement with the prior counsel for the class, the five named plaintiffs had entered into an incentive arrangement whereby class counsel was obligated to seek an incentive payment for each of the five on a sliding scale that was tied to the amount of the settlement. For example, if the settlement amount was greater than or equal to $500,000, class counsel would seek a $10,000 award for each of them; a $25,000 award if it was $1.5 million or more; a $50,000 award if it was $5 million or more; and a $75,000 award if it was $10 million or more. This arrangement was not disclosed at the class certification hearing.

At the final hearing on the settlement's fairness, reasonableness and adequacy, the district court approved the settlement but denied the motion for incentive awards, on the basis that "the amount was unreasonable in light of the work and risk undertaken, and that the incentive agreements created actual conflicts of interest in violation of public policy." The district court also approved class counsel's request for attorney's fees in connection with the settlement. The objectors appealed the district court's approval of the settlement agreement primarily because of the presence of the incentive agreements, which they argued had prevented the class representatives from providing adequate representation to the class as a whole.

Conflict of Interest Created by Structure of Incentive Agreement
The Ninth Circuit upheld the district court's approval of the settlement agreement in spite of the incentive agreements because two of the class representatives and their counsel did not have a fee agreement to receive such incentives. The Ninth Circuit, however, ruled that the incentive agreements created a conflict of interest between the class representatives and the remainder of the class.

Although—according to the Court's opinion—additional payments to class representatives are fairly typical in class action cases to compensate class representatives for work done on behalf of the class, this incentive arrangement was different. *But cf. Oliver v. Boston University*, Delaware Chancery Court, No. 16570-VCN (May 29, 2009), slip op. at 2 (only in exceptional cases should an application for compensation to a representative plaintiff be granted).

Although the granting of a request for incentive awards to class representatives is discretionary, the instant incentive agreements "tied the promised request to the ultimate recovery and in so doing, put class counsel and the contracting class representatives into a conflict position from day one." The Ninth Circuit further reasoned that the structure of such an agreement gave the contracting representatives an interest in only a monetary settlement, as distinguished from other remedies, that set them apart from other members of the class. The court also had a problem with the failure by class counsel to disclose the agreements sooner, and also noted that agreements of this sort: "infect the class action environment with the troubling appearance of shopping plaintiff-ships"; "could tempt potential plaintiffs to sell their lawsuits to attorneys [that] are the highest bidders"; and "implicate California ethics rules that prohibit representation of clients with conflicting interests".

As a result, the Ninth Circuit, among other things, reversed and remanded to the district court the award of attorney's fees to class counsel for consideration of the impact, if any, of the incentive agreements on entitlement to fees. *See generally, Iron Workers Local No. 25 Pension Fund v. Credit-Based Asset Servicing and Securitization, LLC,* S.D. N.Y., 08 Civ. 10841 (JSR) (May 26, 2009) (criticizing conflict issues that arise when class counsel provides portfolio monitoring for the class representatives for whom they file cases.) *Compare, Plumbers, Pipefitters and Apprentices Local 112 Pension Fund v. CIT Group Inc.,* S.D. N.Y., 08 CV 6613 (BSJ), Order, (May 22, 2009) (not finding any conflict issues with class counsel providing portfolio monitoring for class representative for whom they later file class action suits.)

In those cases where the fee arrangement with class counsel is not an issue, the general rule in determining the appropriate award of attorneys' fees in class actions is that the court may consider factors such as: (i) the time and effort devoted to the case by plaintiffs' counsel; (ii) the relative complexities of the litigation; (iii) the skills necessary to pursue the litiga-tion; (iv) whether the fee is contingent; (v) the standing and ability of counsel; and, (vi) the benefit achieved. In addition, when a specific fund is created, tying the fee award to the amount of the recovery is a common practice. *See, In Re Cablevision/Rainbow Media Group Tracking Stock Litigation,* Delaware Chancery Court, No. 19819-VCN (May 22, 2009); *Sugarland Indus., Inc. v. Thomas,* 420 A.2d 142, 149 (Del. 1980).

Lesson to be Learned

This opinion makes it clear that while class counsel can allow for class representatives in a class action to be awarded extra compensation at the court's discretion, they cannot structure a deal where the promise to request the extra award for a class representative is tied to the ultimate monetary amount of the class recovery. Such a structure creates a wedge between the class representative's hope for a personal benefit not shared by the class from a monetary settlement, compared to the goal of what is best for the class as a whole—such as taking the risk of going to trial. This type of fee arrangement creates a conflict of interest and could jeopardize the amount of fees awarded to class counsel in connection with the settlement. The impropriety of such incentive agreements can be exacerbated, as here, by failing to disclose its presence at the class certification hearing. Thus, if there is any question about a fee agreement with class counsel passing muster, disclosure must be made at the earliest appropriate opportunity. ◆

Francis G.X. Pileggi is the founding partner of the Wilmington, Delaware, office of Fox Rothschild LLP. His blog at www.delawarelitigation.com summarizes all the key decisions on corporate and commercial law from the Delaware Court of Chancery and Delaware Supreme Court, and includes posts on legal ethics. His e-mail address is fpileggi@foxrothschild.com. Sheldon K. Rennie is a partner in the Wilmington office of Fox Rothschild LLP. His e-mail is srennie@foxrothschild.com.

What Happens When Lawyers do not Comply with Confidentiality Requirements in a Lawsuit?

A recent decision from the United States Court of Appeals for the Seventh Circuit answered the question about what penalties an attorney may be subject to if a confidentiality order restricting documents is violated in connection with a lawsuit. Although the decision summarized in this short column also involved many other violations, random comparisons with other decisions are provided that involve much less Draconian penalties for breach of confidentiality provisions.

I. Salmeron v. Enterprise Recovery Systems, Inc.

A. Background
In a *qui tam* action involving allegations of fraudulent student loan debt collection practices, the U.S. Court of Appeals for the Seventh Circuit affirmed the district court's decision to dismiss the suit with prejudice as a penalty for the attorney's willful leaking of the opponent's sensitive document. *See Salmeron v. Enter. Recovery Sys.*, 2009 U.S. App. LEXIS 19316 (7th Cir., Aug. 27, 2009).

Rhonda Salmeron filed a suit against her ex-employer, Enterprise Recovery Systems, Inc., alleging that it engaged in fraudulent student loan debt collection practices. Salmeron later amended her complaint to add USA Funds, Inc.; Sallie Servicing L.P.; and others as additional defendants.

During the three years the lawsuit progressed in district court, her attorney repeatedly missed filing deadlines and failed to appear at conferences. Citing personal issues and a heavy workload for the delays, her attorney was granted numerous extensions yet continued to miss the supplemental deadlines. Fed up with the attorney's "virtually unbroken pattern of dilatory and irresponsible conduct," the district court dismissed the suit without prejudice *sua sponte* after the attorney once again failed to timely respond by a third extended deadline. *See U.S. ex rel. Salmeron v. Enter. Recovery Sys.*, 2008 U.S. Dist. LEXIS 73616 (N.D. Ill., Aug. 18, 2008). Although the district court reinstated the suit, it also issued the attorney a "final warning," stating that future misconduct on his behalf would reap serious consequences. Nevertheless, the attorney continued his pattern of misconduct by leaking his opponent's sensitive documents in violation on an "attorneys' eyes only" agreement.

In June 2008, defendants learned that a copy of a confidential document containing the Guarantee Services Agreement between Sallie Mae and USA Funds had been leaked to the Web site Wikileaks.org and the *Chronicle of Higher Education* (the "*Chronicle*"). The leaked document bore a stamp demonstrating that it had come from USA Funds' document production during this suit. USA Funds then moved to dismiss the suit as a penalty for disclosure of the document.

B. Procedural and Factual Setting
During discovery, USA Funds' counsel and plaintiff's counsel agreed to keep the Guarantee Service Agreement confidential based on an "attorneys' eyes only" agreement. The agreement was a temporary measure until the existing protective order could be amended to include all parties and necessary documents. In addition to the "attorneys' eyes only" agreement, USA Funds submitted a draft protective order to the plaintiff's attorney that encompassed the Guarantee Service Agreement; but the plaintiff's attorney failed to return his modifications to the proposed order, and instead divulged the confidential document to third parties.

At the hearing on the motion to dismiss, the plaintiff's attorney admitted to the district court that he disclosed the Guarantee Service Agreement to his client, another attorney, and a *Chronicle* reporter. He also later admitted that if he had referred to the cover letter attached to the document, he would have been aware of the "attorneys' eyes only" agreement. The district court found that he had willfully violated the "attorneys' eyes only" agreement, and dismissed the case with prejudice.

C. Seventh Circuit Decision
Salermon appealed the district court's dismissal of the case to the Seventh Circuit, which affirmed, holding that the district court did not clearly err or abuse its discretion. The court highlighted that the disclosure to the *Chronicle* reporter, which any reasonable person would know would lead to its publication, was more than sufficient to show willfulness.

The court also rejected Salmeron's tandem arguments that the disclosure of the Guarantee Service Agreement was not sanctionable because: (1) no protective order was in place; and (2) the district court had not yet found good cause to keep the document confidential. According to the court, the protective-order process was bypassed when the document was leaked. Thus, according to the court, Salmeron could not complain of a lack of a good cause ruling.

The court further held that USA Funds was not to blame for failing to seek a protective order sooner when it did not promptly hear back from the opposing lawyer. Highlighting the rules of professional conduct, the court noted that attorneys are permitted to take opposing counsel at their word. Thus, USA Funds was entitled to rely upon promises that he would keep the document confidential and respond to the protective order.

Salmeron further complained that she was not adequately warned that dismissal would result from her attorney's disclosure. The court flatly rejected this contention, finding that the earlier dismissal of the lawsuit without prejudice was a "warning shot." The district court adequately apprised the plaintiff's attorney that his further misconduct would result in drastic consequences for him and his client.

Ultimately the Seventh Circuit held that the district court did not clearly err in finding that the attorney willfully leaked the document, nor did it abuse its discretion by dismissing Salermon's suit with prejudice as a penalty for her lawyer's misconduct.

II. Short Comparison of Random Related Cases

A random sampling of other cases that have dealt with the issue of failure to comply with confidentiality agreements or orders in connection with documents produced in litigation include the following. In *eBay Domestic Holdings, Inc. v. Newmark*, No. 3705-CC (Del. Ch., Sept. 16, 2009), the Delaware Court of Chancery allowed for the return or "clawback" of inadvertently produced documents without a waiver of privilege. This case involved not only an issue about which documents were privileged, but also a dispute about

whether certain documents should be designated as merely "confidential" as compared to "highly confidential," the latter designation requiring that the documents would be viewed by outside counsel only, and not their clients, including a prohibition against in-house counsel viewing those documents. Also instructive is *Postorivo v. AG Paintball Holdings, Inc.*, 2008 WL 3876199 (Del. Ch., Aug. 20, 2008), in which the Court recognized that in modern commercial litigation, especially due to the enormous volume of electronic discovery involved, the risk of inadvertent production of confidential or privileged data is great. The 70-page opinion explained in detail various violations by counsel of certain obligations, which included use of privileged data, which the Court explained should result in disqualification of counsel.

By comparison, in *Portnoy v. Cryo-Cell International, Inc.*, 2008 Del. Ch. LEXIS 6 (2008), the Delaware Court of Chancery declined to award some relief that otherwise may have been granted, due in part to the apparent violation of a confidentiality agreement by the plaintiff, who otherwise was given the relief requested in connection with a challenge to the election of directors as a result of the improper actions of management leading up to and during an annual meeting of shareholders. *See generally Southeastern Mechanical Services, Inc. v. Brody*, 2009 WL 2883057 (M.D. Fla. Aug. 31, 2009) (imposing the penalty of an adverse inference for failure to preserve data on the Blackberries of employees of a company that was subject to a TRO). ◆

AUTHOR'S NOTE: Importantly, I would like to thank Maura Burke, a new associate in our firm, for her invaluable contribution to this article.

Francis G.X. Pileggi is the founding partner of the Wilmington, Delaware, office of Fox Rothschild LLP, an AmLaw 200 firm. His blog at www.delawarelitigation.com summarizes all the key decisions on corporate and commercial law from the Delaware Court of Chancery and Delaware Supreme Court, and includes posts on legal ethics and related topics. His e-mail address is: fpileggi@foxrothschild.com.

Attorney/Client Privilege Honored Despite E-mail Communication Sent from Employer's Account

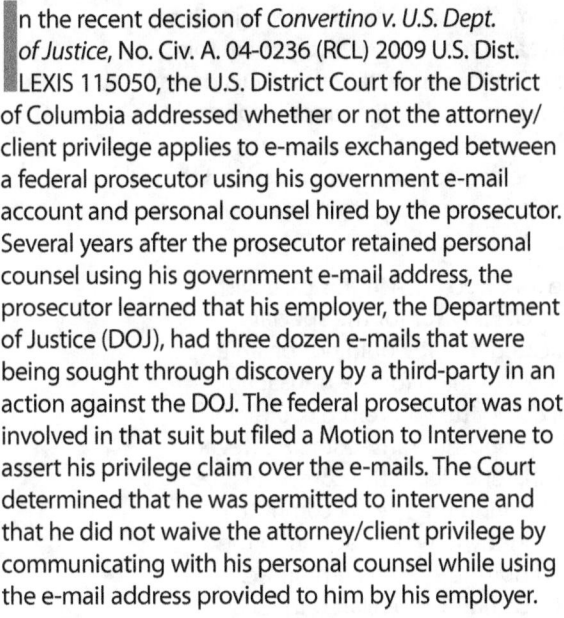

In the recent decision of *Convertino v. U.S. Dept. of Justice*, No. Civ. A. 04-0236 (RCL) 2009 U.S. Dist. LEXIS 115050, the U.S. District Court for the District of Columbia addressed whether or not the attorney/client privilege applies to e-mails exchanged between a federal prosecutor using his government e-mail account and personal counsel hired by the prosecutor. Several years after the prosecutor retained personal counsel using his government e-mail address, the prosecutor learned that his employer, the Department of Justice (DOJ), had three dozen e-mails that were being sought through discovery by a third-party in an action against the DOJ. The federal prosecutor was not involved in that suit but filed a Motion to Intervene to assert his privilege claim over the e-mails. The Court determined that he was permitted to intervene and that he did not waive the attorney/client privilege by communicating with his personal counsel while using the e-mail address provided to him by his employer.

In determining whether or not the privilege was waived due to the e-mails being disclosed to a third-party, the employer, the Court relied on Federal Rule of Evidence 502(b) which provides that no waiver exists if: "(1) The disclosure is inadvertent;" and "(2) The holder of the privilege or protection took reasonable steps to prevent disclosure." The Court reasoned that the disclosure was inadvertent because the prosecutor had no intention of allowing the DOJ, to read the e-mails he sent to his personal attorney using his work e-mail account. The prosecutor, as an employee of the DOJ, failed to realize that the DOJ kept the e-mails even after they were deleted. Once, however, he discovered that the DOJ still had access to the e-mails, he took reasonable steps to prevent disclosure to additional parties by filing a Motion to Intervene.

The employee reasonably expected that his e-mails to his personal attorney would remain confidential. The Court relied on the decision in the case of *In re Asia Global Crossing, Ltd.*, 322 B.R. 247, 258 (S.D.N.Y 2005). In that case, the Court determined that the question of privilege "comes down to whether the intent to communicate in confidence was objectively reasonable." *Id.* In order for documents sent by e-mail to be protected by the attorney/client privilege, there "must be a subjective expectation of confidentiality that is found to be objectively reasonable." *Id.* at 257. The Court outlined four factors to determine reasonableness: "(1) Does the corporation maintain a policy

banning personal or other objectionable use, (2) Does the company monitor the use of their employees' computer or e-mail, (3) Do third-parties have a right of access to the computer or e-mails, and (4) Did the corporation notify the employee, or was the employee aware, of the use and monitoring policies?" *Id.* In this case, the Court reasoned that the expectation of privacy was reasonable. The DOJ maintains a policy that does not ban personal use of company e-mail and although the DOJ does have access to personal e-mails sent through their account, the prosecutor/employee in this case was unaware that the DOJ would be regularly accessing and saving e-mails from his account even after they were deleted. Because the Court reasoned that his expectations were reasonable, the Court concluded that his private e-mails would remain protected by the attorney/client privilege.

There are contrary holdings by other courts that have addressed the same issue but ruled differently than the court in *Convertino*. *See, e.g., Scott v. Beth Israel Medical Center, Inc.*, 17 Misc. 3d 934, 847 N.Y.S. 2d 436 (Sup. 2007). *See generally* Andrew Serwin, *Information Security and Privacy: Practice Guide to Federal, State and International Law* § 9:5 (July 2009); Adam Losey, *Clicking Away Confidentiality: Workplace Waiver of Attorney-Client Privilege*, 60 Fla. L. Rev. 1179 (Dec. 2008); Kara Williams, *Protecting What You Thought was Yours: Expanding Employee Privacy to Protect the Attorney/Client Privilege from Employer Computer Monitoring*, 69 Ohio St. L. J. 347 (2008).

The cases on this issue vary from state to state, without a general rule that can be safely applied nationwide. One writer has summarized a leading case as formulating the following test: "Does the employee know that his/her e-mails are monitored by the company? If so, then there is a strong argument that the attorney/client privilege does not apply because there is no objective or subjective expectation of privacy." *See* Michael Fielding, *Practical Pointers for Your Practice: Bankruptcy, ESI and the Attorney/Client Privilege*, 26-10 Amer. Bank. Inst. J. 52 (Dec. 2007/Jan. 2008) (citing *Curto v. Medical World Communications, Inc.*, 2006 WL 1318387 (S.D.N.Y. 2006)). *See also Sims v. Lakeside School*, 2007 WL 2745367 (W.D.Wash. 2007).

In sum, this is an issue that requires familiarity with state specific statutes and case law. Proceed with caution. ◆

Francis G.X. Pileggi is the founding partner of the Wilmington, DE, office of Fox Rothschild LLP. His blog at www. delawarelitigation. com summarizes all the key decisions on corporate and commercial law from the Delaware Court of Chancery and Delaware Supreme Court, and includes posts on legal ethics and related topics. His e-mail address is: fpileggi@ foxrothschild.com. He is a member of the Herrmann Technology AIC.

Delaware Court of Chancery Affirms Standards for Counsel in Class Actions

The Delaware Court of Chancery in the recent decision of *In Re Revlon, Inc. Shareholders Litigation*, Consol. C.A. No. 4578-VCL (Del. Ch. March 16, 2010), describes the standards of professionalism and fiduciary duties for lawyers that file class actions in Delaware. The specific context of this case involves the common practice of filing lawsuits very soon after the public announcement of a corporate transaction, and the ensuing battle for lead counsel among firms filing competing complaints involving the same contested transaction. Although this opinion is only 44-pages in the slip opinion format, it speaks volumes about the practical and theoretical aspects of representative litigation, as well as the standards that the Court of Chancery enforces on all counsel that appear before it. This case should be read in tandem with the recent Delaware Court of Chancery decision in *State Line Ventures, LLC v. RBS Citizens*, C.A. No. 4705-VCL (Dec. 2, 2009), which described the standards of practice that are expected of Delaware lawyers—in all types of cases, who move the admission *pro hac vice* of attorneys who are not licensed to practice in Delaware. These standards are also of practical importance for the many non-Delaware lawyers that are admitted on a *pro hac vice* basis to practice in Delaware.

The *Revlon* opinion includes scholarly analysis regarding the criteria employed by the court in its selection of lead counsel in class actions, noting that the size of the plaintiff's stock ownership is not always determinative. The court cites to many academic sources that discuss the policy issues that arise in these types of cases, as well as the "pros and cons" of what the court refers to as "entrepreneurial litigators" who have a portfolio of class action cases.

Much of the opinion discusses the types of class actions that arise in the context of what the court referred to as the *Cox Communications* ritual, referring to the case of *In re Cox Communications, Inc.*, 879 A.2d 604, 608 (Del. Ch. 2005). That "ritual" as the Court describes it, involves a common practice in many representative suits that are hastily filed very shortly after the announcement of a controlling shareholder transaction. The court has referred to these hastily prepared and hastily filed complaints as part of the "medal round of filing speed Olympics to seek lead counsel status." The court also cites to a law review article that refers to an academic analysis that concluded: "Firms that are early filers are frequently early settlers," (leading some wags to

label them "Pilgrims.") In addition to referring to it as a ritual, the court also refers to the situation in this case as "part of a Cox Communications Kabuki dance [that] involves two tracks." The first track involves representative counsel doing "not very much" in the litigation, while the controlling shareholder and the special committee for the company move forward along the transactional track.

That procedure followed form in this case with a twist. The financial advisor for the special committee indicated that it would not be able to render a fairness opinion for the transaction and the special committee therefore could not recommend the proposed transaction. However, the controlling shareholder in the company did an "end run" around the special committee by proposing a slightly new transaction to the entire board and not the special committee. Thus, the special committee declared that its work was complete and disbanded. Although the board declined to make any recommendation to stockholders on whether or not to tender their shares, the board did authorize Revlon to proceed with the proposed transaction.

The Litigation Track Restarts and the Parties Enter into a Memorandum of Understanding

The *Cox Communications* ritual was described by the court as follows: Once the corporation and the controlling shareholder reached an unofficial agreement on the terms of the transaction, the plaintiffs were brought in to "bless the deal." The transaction provided for consideration for a settlement and the payment of attorneys' fees and a broad transaction-wide release for all defendants. The minor tweaks in the transaction followed in what the court called this "traditional choreography." The transactional tweak traditionally involves lowering the termination fee that would only become operative in the event of a topping bid and supplemental disclosures that provide convenient ways to settle litigation over a deal that has already been exposed to the market for some time, by which point it is relatively clear to the parties that an interloper is unlikely to appear.

Importantly, one of the tweaks made in this case by the parties was already required by Delaware case law in order to render a controlling stockholder tender offer as non-coercive. The court suggested that such a provision would have been included anyway as a requirement under Delaware law that a controlling stockholder's tender offer be conditioned upon tenders from a majority of the outstanding unaffiliated shares. The *Cox Communications* case is known for requiring that if a tender offer by a controlling shareholder is to be considered non-coercive, when enough shares are tendered such that the remaining holders can be eliminated in a short-form merger, then the squeezed-out stockholders would receive securities in the surviving corporation substantially identical to the shares they would have received. The court regarded the changes to the ultimate terms of the deal as being the result of very little if any influence by the plaintiff's counsel, and the Memorandum of Understanding (MOU) exaggerated the role of counsel in obtaining the proposed settlement. The court refers throughout the opinion to "Old Counsel" as the counsel that it replaced.

New Actions Filed
After the MOU was entered into, new representative actions were filed that challenged the transaction. Unlike the original actions filed by Old Counsel, the new actions challenged an actual transaction. New Counsel argued that there was a conflict between the positions of the tendering stockholders that they represented and the non-tendering stockholders represented by the Old Counsel.

Legal Analysis
The court cites to a treatise and to several federal decisions to support the well-settled principle that the court has both the power and the duty to both select and remove class counsel. Although there may not be substantial case law in the Court of Chancery on this specific topic, comparatively speaking, the court cited to several cases that list the factors important in choosing lead counsel, such as the quality of the pleading, the willingness and ability to litigate vigorously on behalf of an entire class, and the enthusiasm or vigor with which the various contestants have prosecuted the lawsuit. *See Hirt v. U.S. Timberlands Serv. Co.*, 2002 WL 1558342 at *2 (Del. Ch. July 3, 2002) and *Wiehl v. Eon Labs*, 2005 WL 696764, at *1 (Del. Ch. May 22, 2005). Notably, the court emphasized that the size of plaintiff's share ownership is not a determinative factor in selecting lead counsel.

Transaction was not a Voluntary, Non-coercive Tender Offer that Avoided Entire Fairness Review
The court made it clear that this was not a transaction that avoided entire fairness review, based on the case of *In Re Siliconix, Inc. Shareholders Litigation*, 2001 WL 71677 (Del. Ch. June 19, 2001). The

Siliconix case rests in part on the non-involvement of the target board from the Delaware corporate law perspective. Rather, as a series of cases noted, corporate action by the target board takes a transaction out of the *Siliconix* framework. *See A.G. Andra v. Blount*, 772 A.2d 183, 195 n. 30 (Del. Ch. 2000).

The court also noted other reasons why the entire fairness standard would apply to the deal in this case in part because none of the following safe harbor provisions applied: (1) There was no affirmative recommendation from an independent committee of the target board; (2) It was not subject to a non-waivable condition that a majority of outstanding unaffiliated shares tender; and (3) There was no commitment by the controller to effect a prompt back-end merger. Moreover, in this case the outside directors believed that they could not obtain a fairness opinion for the deal. The court observed that if there was ever a case that warranted the entire fairness review standard, this may be one of those cases.

Policy Considerations
The court recognized the important role of representative cases as a check on management, and that many cases achieve meaningful results. The court recognized also the sound policy reasons for the court to police representative counsel. This opinion made it clear that the court will act as a very "strict policeman," even though the court recognizes that one possible consequence of that approach would be that "frequent filers" may accelerate their efforts to populate their portfolio of cases by filing in other jurisdictions. The court recognized also that while "in the short run policing frequent filers may cost some members of the bar financially, in the long run it enhances the legitimacy of our state and its law not to facilitate a system of transactional insurance through quasi-litigation."

Postscript
As a closing note, it should be observed that in hearings after this decision was rendered, in two separate cases, the court made a point to emphasize that its decision in this case should not be interpreted in a manner that would either disqualify or cast aspersions on the firms involved for purposes of their role in future litigation. *See New Jersey Carpenters Annuity Fund v. Smith International Inc.*, C.A. No. 5259-VCL (Del. Ch. March 19, 2010) (Transcript); *In Re Zenith National Insurance Corp. Shareholders Litigation*, Cons. C.A. No. 5296-VCL (Del. Ch. March 19, 2010)(Transcript). ◆

Francis G.X. Pileggi is the founding partner of the Wilmington, Delaware, office of Fox Rothschild LLP, an AmLaw 200 firm. He maintains a blog at www.delawarelitigation.com. He is a member of the Richard K. Herrmann Technology AIC in Wilmington.

Second Circuit Disqualifies Law Firm for Representation Adverse to Client's Subsidiary

A parent company and its subsidiary may be considered one client for disqualification purposes, and may be the basis for disqualifying a law firm that represents the parent company but at the same time is adverse to that subsidiary in concurrent representation. This was the reasoning of the U.S. Court of Appeals for the Second Circuit in *GSI Commerce Solutions, Inc. v. BabyCenter, L.L.C.*, __ F.3d __, 2010 WL 3239436 (2d Cir. 2010).

Background

BabyCenter, L.L.C. is a wholly-owned subsidiary of Johnson & Johnson, Inc. ("J&J"). The law firm involved in this case represented J&J at the same time it represented GSI Commerce Solutions, Inc. in litigation adverse to BabyCenter. J&J, which the law firm represented in other ongoing but unrelated matters, and BabyCenter objected to the representation of GSI by the law firm. The U.S. District Court for the Southern District of New York disqualified the law firm from the concurrent representation and the Second Circuit affirmed.

J&J entered into a fee agreement with the law firm in which the law firm defined the scope of its representation as limited to compliance matters involving data protection regulations in the European Union. This agreement specifically provided that J&J waived any conflicts related to the law firm's potential adverse representation in patent litigation for Kimberly-Clark that may have been adverse to an affiliate of J&J named McNeil PPC, Inc. In addition to waiving potential conflicts regarding patent matters for Kimberly-Clark, J&J also had agreed to a "standard addendum" in the fee letter that clarified that the representation of J&J by the law firm did not include a representation of any of its affiliates or subsidiaries, directors, officers, members, or any other variations or agents of the parent entity. It also clarified that the attorney-client relationship will be deemed terminated upon the completion of the limited engagement whether or not a letter was sent to confirm the termination of the representation. Nonetheless, the law firm did represent BabyCenter in privacy-related matters although that representation was unrelated to the litigation involving an E-Commerce Services Agreement between BabyCenter and GSI, which is the subject of the litigation about which the disqualification motion pertains. The court also observed that the law firm did not appear to receive any confidential information relevant to the agreement between BabyCenter and GSI.

The court found that BabyCenter shared the same legal department as J&J and it also relied on J&J for accounting, audit, cash management, employee benefits, finance, human resources, information technology, insurance, payroll, and travel services.

Analysis

Relying on several decisions from the Second Circuit, the court stated that the mere violation of the state disciplinary codes would not necessarily warrant disqualification. Rather, disqualification would be warranted only if the "attorney's conduct tends to taint the underlying trial." One established ground for disqualification is concurrent representation of one existing client in a matter adverse to another existing client. (citing *Cinema 5, Ltd. v. Cinerama, Inc.*, 528 F.2d 1384, 1387 (2d Cir. 1976)). The court referred to the ABA Model Rule of Professional Conduct 1.7, comment 34 (2006), for the position that a "lawyer who represents a corporation or other organization does not, by virtue of that representation, necessarily represent any constituent or affiliated organization, such as a parent or subsidiary." This comment refers to the "entity theory" of representation but the comment also notes that an attorney may not accept representation adverse to the affiliate of a client if "circumstances are such that the affiliate should also be considered a client of the lawyer...." *Id.*

The court concluded that the focus in the analysis should be "on the reasonableness of the client's belief that counsel cannot maintain the duty of undivided loyalty it owes a client in one matter while simultaneously opposing that client's corporate affiliate in another." (citations omitted.) The factors considered by other courts in determining whether a corporate affiliate conflict exists include the following: (i) the degree of operational commonality between affiliated entities; and (ii) the extent to which one depends financially on the other. Other courts have suggested that the status of an affiliate as a wholly-owned subsidiary of the client may suffice to establish a corporate affiliate conflict. (citing *Carlyle Towers Condo Association, Inc. v. Crossland Savings, FSB*, 944 F.Supp. 341, 346 (D.N.J. 1996)).

In the instant case, the court reasoned that BabyCenter substantially relied on J&J for an extensive array of services and support. Second, the court relied on the fact that both entities use the same in-house legal department to handle their legal affairs, and a member of the legal department from J&J serves on the board of BabyCenter. Finally, the court emphasized that BabyCenter is a wholly-owned subsidiary of J&J.

Importantly, the court also concluded that J&J did not waive the corporate affiliate conflict as part of the fee agreement with the law firm, despite a related limited waiver that did not apply to the subsidiary or the issue involved in this case. Although the court referred to some commentary and cases that allowed a waiver of a conflict involving a subsidiary, no such waiver was clearly obtained in this matter.

The court concluded by explaining that the representation of an existing client adverse to the subsidiary of another existing client implicates the duty of loyalty, and there was no waiver of that duty that would prevent disqualification here.

Comparison
Other courts have reached similar conclusions when a law firm did not obtain the necessary waiver in connection with claims against an affiliate of a company that the firm had represented. See *Board of Managers of Eleventh Street Loftominium Association v. Wabash Loftominium LLC*, 2007 WL 2416817 (Ill. App. 1 Dist. Aug. 27, 2007). But compare, *Boston Scientific Corporation v. Johnson & Johnson, Inc.*, 647 F.Supp.2d 369 (D. Del. 2009) (court denied a motion to disqualify a law firm from representing Boston Scientific in claims against Wyeth despite the same firm's representation of Wyeth subsidiaries in other matters and reasoned that despite violation of Rule 1.7, disqualification was not warranted.) See *Elonix I.P. Holdings, Ltd. v. Apple Computer, Inc.*, 142 F.Supp.2d 579 (D. Del. 2001) (separate offices of same large firm representing and suing international corporation in unrelated matters, would not be disqualified on conflict of interest basis.) See generally *PharmAthen, Inc. v. SIGA Technologies, Inc.*, 2009 WL 2031793 (Del. Ch. July 10, 2009) (court focused on contacts between the client and the lawyer to determine whether it was reasonable for the client to believe that the attorney was acting on its behalf as counsel in the absence of a formal retainer agreement.)

Although it was mentioned in the opinion, the court in the GSI case did not devote a substantial portion of its analysis to addressing the factors that would warrant disqualification even if the applicable Rules of Professional Conduct were violated. Some of the Delaware decisions cited above focus substantially on that aspect of a motion to disqualify counsel. It is not clear whether Delaware courts would reach the same conclusion as the GSI court. ◆

Francis G.X. Pileggi is the founding partner of the Wilmington, Delaware, office of Fox Rothschild LLP, an AmLaw 200 firm. His blog at www.delawarelitigation.com summarizes all the key decisions on corporate and commercial law from the Delaware Court of Chancery and Delaware Supreme Court.

R.I. Supreme Court Rules that a Law Firm Must be Allowed to Withdraw from Representing Client with Unpaid Legal Bills Despite Looming Trial Date

The Rhode Island Supreme Court reversed a trial court decision that had denied a Motion to Withdraw filed by counsel whose client had a substantial unpaid bill, in an opinion that should be welcomed by all lawyers who prefer not to be forced to work for free (as compared to voluntary *pro bono* work). *See King v. NAIAD Inflatables of Newport, Inc.*, R.I., No. 2009-Appeal (Dec. 14, 2010). The trial court based its decision in large measure on the fact that there was an imminent trial date and it would be difficult for the client to find new counsel without a postponement of the trial date. The supreme court rejected that reasoning.

Factual Background

The underlying case in which the motion was filed dealt with a claim against a company by an independent contractor for sales commissions. The law firm representing the defendant company had been paid on a timely basis for the initial two years that it had been representing the company in the matter but during the last year of the representation, including the year in which a trial was set, the client had been woefully delinquent in paying its bills. The law firm for the delinquent client had a fee agreement in place that provided that bills were payable upon receipt and that the law firm reserved the right to withdraw if bills were not promptly paid. After a lengthy period of dunning proved unproductive, and the law firm faced the prospect of a trial of two weeks in duration, which would naturally make the amount unpaid even larger, a Motion to Withdraw as counsel was filed. Ample notice of the motion was given to the client. The trial court emphasized in its denial of the motion that it would be difficult to maintain the trial date if the motion were granted. Neither opposing counsel nor the delinquent client, however, opposed the Motion to Withdraw.

Reasoning of the Supreme Court

Although the supreme court acknowledged the understandable concern that the trial court had for maintaining its trial calendar, the reversal focused on Rule of Professional Conduct 1.16, which allows for the withdrawal of counsel when the financial obligations of a client are not being fulfilled. The court also relied on the terms of the fee agreement, which provided for withdrawal when, as in this case, the client was not paying its fees when due. It was also important to the supreme court that neither the opposing counsel nor the client opposed the Motion to Withdraw, and that the client had been given fair notice prior to the motion being filed. Perhaps of greater importance to the reasoning of the Rhode Island Supreme Court was that the law firm should not be subjected to undue financial hardship. In addition to the substantial unpaid bills at the time the motion was filed, the law firm was being faced with the unhappy prospect of not being paid for the scheduled two-week trial.

The supreme court reasoned that lawyers are entitled to be paid for their services, similar to other occupations, and should not be forced to work for free. This decision should be music to the ears of lawyers who seek to have removed from their shoulders the yoke of clients who do not pay their bills. It is comforting that the Supreme Court of Rhode Island recognized the unfairness of refusing to remove that burden notwithstanding an imminent trial date. *See generally, Parfi Holding AB v. Mirror Image Internet, Inc.*, 926 A.2d 1071 (Del. 2007) (explaining that a court could not require an attorney to submit a "non-withdrawable entry of appearance," noting the Rule of Professional Conduct that requires an attorney to withdraw in certain circumstances.)

The Model Rules of Professional Conduct were changed in 2002 so that Rule 1.16(b) was renumbered to highlight the point that a lawyer may withdraw for any reason as long as it does not cause a material adverse effect on the interest of the client. The Model Rules follow the traditional view allowing withdrawal if the client fails to fulfill an "obligation" regarding the representation, such as a refusal to make or secure the payment of attorneys' fees and expenses. *See ABA/BNA Lawyers' Manual of Professional Conduct*, Section 31:1108 (January 2010). *See also* G. Hazard and W. Hodes, *The Law of Lawyering*, § 20.9 (3d ed. 2001 & Supp. 2005-2) (Rule 1.16 allows lawyer to withdraw after giving reasonable warning and perhaps providing a reasonable grace period).

This short overview of a relatively short decision should be a basis for optimism to the extent that some courts still are sensitive to the practical realities of practicing law. This sensitivity is consistent with maintaining high professional standards. ◆

Francis G.X. Pileggi is the founding partner of the Wilmington, Delaware, office of Fox Rothschild LLP. He maintains a blog at www.delawarelitigation.com. He writes the ethics column for every other issue of The Bencher. I would like to thank Austen C. Endersby for his contribution to this article.

ETHICS COLUMN
Francis G.X. Pileggi, Esquire

Fifth Circuit Court of Appeals Requires District Judge to Lift Imposition of Sanctions and Orders a Different Judge to Hear Case

The U.S. Court of Appeals for the Fifth Circuit in an unpublished per curiam decision, recently reversed a decision of a district judge in Texas who imposed sanctions on local counsel and out-of-state counsel as well as their client, in connection with a *sua sponte* order challenging statements that the client made, and that the local counsel and out-of-state counsel admitted *pro hac vice*, had argued. *In re: Cleveland*, 5th Cir, No. 11-10039, April 4, 2011 (unpublished), 27 *Law. Man. Prof. Conduct* 220 (April 13, 2011). The court of appeals, in a three-page order, concluded the trial judge should have disqualified himself from the hearing and the decision on sanctions due to his decision being based on the judge's personal knowledge about the facts in dispute. The Fifth Circuit found that "the entirety of the conduct at issue was based on whether or not the district judge said and did the things of which" the client accused him of, and the propriety of the arguments of the lawyers based on their client's testimony in connection with a motion for recusal. The district judge had "taken judicial notice" about whether he made the statements that were attributed to him, and his decision imposing sanctions was based on that "judicial notice."

The appeals court relied on 28 U.S.C. § 455(b)(1) which provides that a federal judge "shall…disqualify himself…[w]here he has…personal knowledge of disputed evidentiary facts concerning the proceeding." The court of appeals observed that the trial judge "repeatedly questioned the witnesses about the judge's own statements and conduct." On remand the fifth circuit appointed a different judge to hear the matter. The ruling vacated the sanctions, which had included disciplinary referrals, because the district judge was disqualified from imposing the sanctions.

This short ruling, which according to Fifth Circuit Rule 47.5 is not precedential, nonetheless exemplifies a thorny conundrum that lawyers face when confronted with the possibility of arguing that a judge should be recused. Another aspect of this decision highlights the risks that may arise in connection with the relationship between local counsel and out-of-state counsel. Although one decision in New Jersey found that local counsel was not responsible for the actions of out-of-state counsel, *see Maldonado v. State*, 225 F.R.D. 120 (D.N.J. 2004) (rejecting *per se* rule penalizing local counsel for out of state counsel's wrongful behavior), the Delaware courts, for example, have been much more demanding and have emphasized the need for local counsel in Delaware to regulate the behavior of out-of-state counsel. Multiple Delaware decisions in which the courts have revoked *pro hac vice* admissions and otherwise suggested that local counsel are responsible for making sure that out-of-state counsel comply with applicable Delaware practice and procedural obligations, were compiled by the Honorable Andrea Rocanelli, former chief counsel for the Office of Disciplinary Counsel of the Supreme Court of Delaware, and now a member of the Delaware judiciary. That compilation is available at the following link: http://www.delawarelitigation.com/2008/01/articles/commentary/delaware-litigation-via-pro-hac-vice-admissions/.

Even when an attorney is admitted *pro hac vice*, Delaware courts require that all court filings and contact with the court be submitted by Delaware local counsel exclusively. *See, e.g., Forte Capital Partners, LLC v. Bennett*, Del. Ch., C.A. No. 1448-N (2005) (court rejected filings signed by Delaware counsel's out-of-state colleague in different office of same firm); and *In re: Member of the Delaware Bar*, Board Case No. 46, 2005, Private Admonition with conditions imposed May 10, 2006 (Trouble ensued when colleague of Delaware lawyer in out-of-state office of same firm, improperly communicated directly with court by phone and in writing. The Court of Chancery referred the matter to Disciplinary Counsel.)

In sum, this ruling by the Fifth Circuit might serve as a reminder of the dangers associated with trying to recuse a judge or moving the admission *pro hac vice* of other lawyers. ◆

Francis G.X. Pileggi created and maintains the Delaware Corporate and Commercial Litigation Blog at www.delawarelitigation.com. In May 2011 he joined Eckert Seamans Cherin & Mellott LLC as the partner in charge of their Delaware office. He is a Master of the Bench in the Richard K. Herrmann Technology AIC in Wilmington, Delaware.

The Moral Aspect of a Lawyer's Fiduciary Duty

It remains axiomatic that lawyers acting on behalf of clients are subject to exacting duties of a fiduciary nature. *See* Geoffrey Hazard, Jr. and W. William Hodes, 1 *The Law of Lawyering*, §4.12 (3d ed) (citing Restatement of the Law Governing Lawyers, §56, Comment b). *See generally*, Restatement of the Law Governing Lawyers, §2, Comment d (referring to requirement of good moral character for admission to bar in most states).

The standard applicable to a fiduciary encompasses a "legal or moral recognition of trust, reliance, or dependence," Sarah W. Holtman, "Fiduciary Relationships," *The Encyclopedia of Ethics*, 545-49 (2nd ed. 2001). *See generally*, Stephen Bainbridge, "Catholic Social Thought and the Corporation" (2003) (discussing influence of Catholic theology on corporate governance), available at: *http://papers. ssrn.com/sol3/papers.cfm?abstract_id=461100*.

Formulations of the key aspects of fiduciary duties include the well-known definition by Judge Benjamin Cardozo as the Chief Judge of the New York Court of Appeals in the 1928 case of *Meinhard v. Salmon*, in which he insists that: (i) fiduciaries must be held to a higher standard than what is applicable to the normal marketplace transaction; (ii) exceptions to this standard undermine the duty of loyalty; and (iii) neither courts nor regulators should consciously weaken the fiduciary standard.

The religious origin of fiduciary principles has been traced to both the Old and New Testaments. *See* Susan Atherton, et al., "Fiduciary Principles: Corporate Responsibilities to Stakeholders", 2 *Journal of Religion and Business Ethics*, 8 (2011). Fiduciary law is traceable to developments in ancient Roman law and early English law which defined fiduciary relationships as both moral and legal relationships of trust. *Id.* at 10. *See generally*, Charles Fried, "The Lawyer as Friend, The Moral Foundation of the Lawyer-Client Relationship", 85 *Yale L.J.* 1060 (1976).

In a secular and pluralistic society such as the United States, it may be controversial in some circles to talk of morality as a basis of fiduciary duties, where there may be contested views of what constitutes moral behavior. For example, Stephen Gillers has argued that: "When lawyers act within the rights-adjudicating apparatus…, its cloak of legitimacy should insulate them against charges of immorality based on a client's ends." Stephen Gillers, "Can a Good Lawyer Be a Bad Person", 2 *J. Inst. for Study of Legal Ethics*, 131, 147 (1999). Still another respected writer on the topic of legal ethics, Monroe Freedman, has urged that: lawyers have a moral obligation of justification for actions they take on behalf of clients, which (I would add), includes actions taken in furtherance of their fiduciary duties. *See* Monroe H. Freedman, "The Lawyer's Moral Obligation of Justification", 74 *Tex. L. Rev.* 111 (1995).

Some writers propose that agreeing to represent a client carries with it the possibility of interfering with the moral autonomy of the lawyer. *See* Judith McMorrow and Luke Scheuer, "The Moral Responsibility of the Corporate Lawyer," Boston College Law School Faculty Paper, 29 (2010), available at *http://lawdigitalcommons.bc.edu/lsfp/268*. Other legal ethics experts advance the position that a lawyer's advice should include a discussion of the moral dimensions of the means and ends of a client's project. *Id.* (citing Thomas L. Shaffer and Robert F. Cochran, Jr., *Lawyers, Clients and Moral Responsibility* (1994)). *See generally* J. Ratnaswamy, "The Lawyer as Moral Actor and the ABA Model Rules," *The Bencher* (January/February 2012).

Even in our increasingly secular world, respected members of our profession still maintain the position that "lawyers must assume moral responsibility for the consequences of their professional actions." Deborah Rhode, "Ethical Perspectives on Legal Practice", 37 *Stan. L. Rev.* 389, 643 (1985).

Prof. Larry Ribstein has published extensive scholarship on the fiduciary duty of partners, which I cannot do justice to in this short essay. *See generally*, *Bromberg and Ribstein on Partnership*, (Aspen Publishers 2011). I am certain that my recently departed learned friend would have commented nonetheless on this short ethics column but for his untimely passing. The legal profession has suffered a great loss with his death.

Consistent with a lawyer's duty to comply with positive civil law, a lawyer's fiduciary duty to act in the best interests of those on whose behalf the lawyer is acting, remains consistent with Judeo-Christian altruistic principles on which our country and its legal system were founded, and on which the basic concept of fiduciary obligation is grounded. It remains helpful to examine the origins of a duty in order to understand it better. So too, an appreciation of the moral aspects of fiduciary duty should illuminate its contours. ◆

Francis G.X. Pileggi is the Member-in-Charge of the Wilmington, Delaware, office of Eckert Seamans Cherin & Mellott, LLC. His e-mail address is fpileggi@ eckertseamans. com. He summarizes the corporate and commercial decisions of Delaware Courts, as well as providing commentaries on legal ethics, at www. delawarelitigation. com. He is a member of the Richard K. Herrmann Technology AIC.

Resources for Legal Ethics Research and Analysis

Over the last 15 years or so that I have been writing this ethics column, I often summarize recent decisions involving legal ethics or professional responsibility that may have some educational value to the national readership of this publication. In the course of doing so for this article, I was reminded of the voluminous number of resources available to those who need to research or analyze an issue of legal ethics. I decided to use this column to provide an overview of the key sources available on the rules of professional conduct and other materials that govern the conduct of lawyers.

For example, in Delaware, the website of the Office of Disciplinary Counsel, a branch of the Delaware Supreme Court that investigates complaints against lawyers, has a link to the decisions of the Delaware Supreme Court involving public and private reprimands, as well as a *Digest of Lawyer Discipline*, which has a link to the decisions of the Court in which public discipline has been imposed on a Delaware lawyer. (This and other links are easily found by performing a Google search.) In addition, the Delaware State Bar Association has a link on its website to the opinions of the Bar Association's Committee on Professional Ethics, which issues non-binding opinions at the request of members of the Delaware Bar. The Bar Association Committee also provides commentary on proposed changes to the Rules of Professional Conduct. This committee is separate from the Delaware Supreme Court's Permanent Advisory Committee on the Delaware Rules of Professional Conduct. The Delaware State Bar Association website also includes a link to ethics columns by Charles Slanina, whose column is published each month in a Bar Association newsletter. (The ethics columns from this publication are available at www.innsofcourt.org/TheBencher).

From a national perspective, there are several online gateways and research guides that provide an extensive list of the materials available to help locate opinions and secondary sources covering legal ethics. Georgetown Law has an online Legal Ethics Research Guide, which reminds the reader to consult sources beyond the familiar cases and statutes, such as Codes of Professional Ethics, as well as ethics opinions issued by state and national bar associations. Other secondary sources include blogs, books, multi-volume treatises and articles. Among the most comprehensive of secondary sources is the *ABA/BNA Lawyers' Manual on Professional Conduct*, which includes the full text of the Rules of Professional Conduct in their various versions for each state, and extensive citations to cases, articles, and books discussing the issues arising under each rule. Also useful is the *National Reporter on Legal Ethics and Professional Responsibility*, edited by Roy M. Mersky and Norman Quist. A helpful treatise is Geoffrey C. Hazard & W. William Hodes, *The Law of Lawyering* (3d ed. 2001), and also notable is Robert H. Aronson & Donald T. Weckstein, *Legal Ethics in a Nutshell* (3d ed. 2007). An essential resource in this area is the *Restatement of the Law Third: The Law Governing Lawyers* (2000).

Among the sites that provide commentary and analysis on legal ethics issues are legalethics.com, Legal Ethics Forum, as well as the ABA Center for Professional Responsibility. The latter provides, in addition to publications and opinions, an online research service that offers guidance on ethical dilemmas and assists in identifying appropriate standards and materials to address those dilemmas. Another online resource is *Freivogel on Conflicts*, which provides frequently updated materials on ethics-related topics.

Other helpful online research gateways include a website sponsored by the University of San Francisco School of Law that provides a link to *The Notre Dame Journal of Law, Ethics and Public Policy*; *Georgetown Journal of Legal Ethics*; and *The Journal of the Legal Profession*. The Cornell Law School Legal Ethics Library is also a valuable online compilation with a comprehensive collection of resources for researching legal ethics topics.

Finally, one can follow the conventional procedures for researching court decisions that address legal ethics such as searches via Lexis and Westlaw. The limits of relying only on trial court decisions in this area may be reflected in Delaware cases, for example, where the trial courts often observe that their primary obligation is not to enforce the Rules of Professional Conduct. *See, e.g., Manning v. Vellardita*, C.A. No. 6812-VCG (Del. Ch. March 28, 2012) (denying a motion to disqualify counsel but referring the attorney involved to the appropriate agencies in Delaware and New York to investigate an apparent violation of Lawyers' Rule of Professional Conduct 1.9) (decision available at www.delawarelitigation.com). ◆

Francis G.X. Pileggi is the Member-in-Charge of the Wilmington, Delaware, office of Eckert Seamans Cherin & Mellott, LLC. He summarizes the corporate and commercial decisions of Delaware Courts, and provides commentaries on legal ethics, at www.delawarelitigation.com.

Court Penalizes Attorney for Faulty Case Citation and Failure to Address Adverse Authority

An attorney was fined in a recent Delaware opinion for misrepresenting what a key case stood for, as well as failing to address adverse opinions in response to a motion for summary judgment. While the attorney contended that his misstatement and lack of reference to opposing authority were good faith mistakes and due to unawareness of adverse rulings, the trial court felt these missteps were not only unacceptable, but tainted the fairness and efficiency of the court. *In re Asbestos Litigation,* C.A. No. 09C-11-059 ASB (Del. Super. Ct. Oct. 28, 2011). As of this writing, the case is pending on appeal before the Delaware Supreme Court.

Delaware Rule of Professional Conduct 3.3(a)(1) states that a lawyer must not knowingly make a false statement of material fact or law, and while this cannot be violated through mere negligence; reckless conduct may satisfy the rule's knowledge requirement. The standard may include turning a blind eye to the obvious, ignoring what there is a duty to see, or declaring as fact something an attorney knows nothing about. *Office of Disciplinary Counsel v. Price,* 732 A.2d 599, 604 (Pa. 1999). While there are good faith mistakes, lawyers must not file briefs or pleadings that contain allegations or statements that they know to be false, or misrepresent material facts or law. *In re Kalal,* 643 N.W.2d 466, 468-74 (Wis. 2002). A lawyer who deliberately misleads a court violates Rule 3.3(a)(1) even if the statement is literally true and therefore not "false." *Texas-Ohio Gas, Inc. v. Mecom,* 28 S.W.3d 129, 145 (Tex. App. 2000).

Everyone makes mistakes. The issue in this context is how to determine which mistakes should be penalized. The Delaware case of *In re Asbestos Litigation* involved a response to a summary judgment motion in which the plaintiff's counsel asserted that the court had previously denied (in another case) the same defendant's motion for summary judgment on weaker facts than were being presented, and cited to a case. However the case counsel cited was the wrong case, and had in fact, been settled prior to an argument on the motion. After the court became aware that the citation was to the wrong case, the court issued an Order to Show Cause as to why the falsity of the statement did not warrant sanctions under Superior Court Civil Rule 11(b). In counsel's response to the court's Order to Show Cause, counsel admitted the error but contended that sanctions were not appropriate because the mistakes were made in good faith and the case that was accidently cited to "seemed to be the most likely case." *In re Asbestos Litigation,* C.A. No. 09C-11-059 ASB at 4. In a second response issued two days later, counsel identified the correct case, and due to the similarities in the cases, argued that sanctions were not appropriate because a Rule 11 violation is determined by a subjective good faith test; and he pleaded, misstatements committed in subjective good faith are not enough to satisfy a Rule 11 violation. *See generally Policemen's Annuity and Benefit Fund v. DV Realty Advisors LLC,* C.A. No. 7204-VCN (Del. Ch. Aug. 16, 2012) (comparing common law definition of good faith in fiduciary duty context and contract law context).

The court in the case of *In re Asbestos Litigation* reasoned that even when an attorney subsequently corrects an errant pleading, the submission of inaccurate and unverified authorities initially, expecting that the court would rely on them, was unacceptable, and identifying the correct case subsequently does not cleanse the sin. The court emphasized that the ease with which counsel found the correct cite strengthened the court's suspicions that no real attempt to ensure the accuracy of the original citation was made. *Id.* at 5. The court further explained that in this situation counsel failed to conduct thorough research. Counsel claimed that a good faith test is required, but the court noted that current Delaware law looks to the reasonableness under the circumstances in determining whether an attorney's actions warrant sanctions. *Id.* at 4. The court held that once Rule 11 violations have been committed, a penalty should follow. *Id.* at 5.

The court also focused on counsel's failure to cite and address adverse legal authorities. Three adverse cases were cited in the defendant's motion for summary judgment, and plaintiff's counsel was presented with copies of those decisions. But in the opposition briefs of the plaintiff's counsel (the one who was fined), none of the cases was referenced. *Id.* Initially, plaintiff's counsel responded that he was unaware of the three prior decisions, which the court found to be unreasonable since they had been cited in the motion for summary judgment, copies were attached to the motion, the plaintiff's counsel's firm was the counsel of record, and in the response, counsel for the plaintiff noted that he was aware of the court's prior decisions. *Id.* In an alternative argument, plaintiff's counsel contends that the cases are not controlling law and therefore there was no obligation to disclose them, but the court was not convinced. The court ruled that the three cases needed to be presented at least in order to distinguish them from the case plaintiff's counsel presented, and that by ignoring those decisions, counsel violated his professional responsibility. *Id.* The court held that the plaintiff's attorney's decision not to address adverse rulings was an intentional act to mislead the court. The court underscored its view that a critical duty of an attorney is to distinguish adverse authority, and ignoring that duty "fits precisely into the language of Rule 11(b)(2) and demonstrates exactly why the Rule exists." *Id.* at 8. Although this decision is the subject of a pending appeal, it serves as a cautionary tale for those submitting written legal arguments to Delaware courts. ◆

Francis G.X. Pileggi is the Member-in-Charge of the Wilmington, Delaware, office of Eckert Seamans Cherin & Mellott, LLC. He summarizes the corporate and commercial decisions of Delaware Courts and provides commentaries on legal ethics at www.delawarelitigation.com.

Delaware Supreme Court Clarifies Standards for Enforcement of Legal Ethics and Attorney Conduct

In my last ethics column, I discussed a trial court opinion that imposed penalties on a lawyer for not citing applicable authority in a brief, and for not accurately describing another case cited in a brief. See my November/December 2012 column in *The Bencher* available at the following link: www.innsofcourt.org/ethicsND2012. This current column is about a review of that decision by the Delaware Supreme Court in an opinion that establishes new rules and standards that will now apply in Delaware when trial judges seek to penalize lawyers for "not following the rules" of legal ethics and civil procedure.

The Delaware Supreme Court opinion in *Crumplar v. The Superior Court of the State of Delaware*, 2012 WL 5194074 (Del. Supr. 2012), involves the appeal by an attorney of a penalty, or sanction, imposed by the trial judge for what the trial judge regarded as a violation of the rules applicable to lawyer conduct. In brief, the trial court imposed a penalty of $25,000 on the attorney for: (i) citing to an incorrect case name and citation for an otherwise accurate statement; and (ii) failure to discuss or distinguish applicable trial court authority raised in an opponent's motion.

Highlights of Legal Principles Promulgated
This opinion by Delaware's High Court announces new guidance for the application of Rule 11. The Delaware Rules of Civil Procedure track the federal rules, and federal cases construing Delaware's version of Rule 11 are often persuasive.

Rule 11, in sum, prevents an attorney from filing papers with the court that are not supported by good faith arguments. This decision establishes that an objective test applies to a review of an attorney's conduct to determine compliance with this rule. That is, the judge should measure the reasonableness of an attorney's conduct based on objective criteria, as opposed to an attorney's subjective "internal belief".

The Supreme Court explained that because an objective standard must be used to determine sanctions under Rule 11: "Delaware demands more from attorneys than pure hearts and empty heads." *Id.* at *5. In other words, "innocent mistakes" in terms of the absence of ill-will, may still be subject to Rule 11 penalties. Delaware's High Court clarified that "the attorney's duty is one of reasonableness under the circumstances; an attorney's subjective good-faith belief in the propriety of his actions does not alone satisfy Rule 11." *Id.* So, even if the

attorney did not intend any harm, she may not be free of culpability. However, "an attorney who fails to respond directly to an opponent's citation of contrary Superior Court cases does not *ipso facto* face Rule 11 sanctions."

Standing
Delaware has long held that non-client litigants should not be allowed to use the allegation of a legal ethics violation to "retaliate" against an opposing lawyer. This addresses non-clients who seek to use arguments about legal ethics in a manner akin to a terrorist's tool.

A non-client litigant, moreover, does not have standing to argue that opposing counsel should be disqualified because of a conflict of interest. *See In Re Infotechnology*, 582 A.2d 215, 218 (Del. 1990). This concept is well-settled in Delaware, but that concept is now extended. In order for disqualification to be appropriate, "the litigant must show that the conflict prejudiced the fairness of the proceeding, not merely that a violation of the Rules had occurred".

This protects against parties who are officious intermeddlers and are more concerned with attacking opposing counsel than enforcing proper attorney conduct. *See generally* footnote 43 (citing to case supporting prejudice when an attorney was both a witness and trial counsel).

In Delaware, trial judges have no independent authority to enforce the Rules of Professional Conduct absent conduct that "prejudicially disrupts the proceeding." This limits the ability of Delaware trial judges to penalize attorneys for violation of the Rule of Professional Conduct.

Rule 11 violations in Delaware, henceforth, cannot be the basis for attorney sanctions if a trial judge believes an attorney has committed misconduct "in the absence of prejudicial disruption of the proceeding." In light of the Supreme Court's exclusive power to supervise the practice of law in Delaware and enforce the Rules of Professional Conduct, the trial judge's proper course of action is to refer the matter to the Office of Disciplinary Counsel, an arm of the Delaware Supreme Court.

For a comparison of a recent federal court in Delaware applying Rule 11, see *Grynberg v. Total*

Compagnie Francaise Des Petroles, 2012 WL 4095186 (D. Del. 2012).

Due Process Requirement for Penalties Imposed on Lawyers by Trial Judge

The Delaware Supreme Court in this opinion also announces a new standard of fairness in Rule 11 matters in which a trial court seeks to impose sanctions on an attorney *sua sponte*. Trial judges must enter an order describing the specific conduct that appears to violate Rule 11. Moreover, trial judges who unilaterally seek to impose Rule 11 sanctions on an attorney pursuant to Rule 11(c)(1) (B) need to comply with the following standard: "A

'reasonable opportunity to respond' when a court invokes Rule 11 (c)(1)(B) should include an opportunity for the attorney to present evidence and respond orally before a court imposes sanctions," 2012 WL 5194074 at *8. Thus, a new dawn emerges in Delaware that clarifies the ground rules for trial judges who seek to penalize lawyers for violations of the rules and arms lawyers with due process rights to defend themselves. ◆

Francis G.X. Pileggi is the Member-in-Charge of the Wilmington, Delaware, office of Eckert Seamans Cherin & Mellott, LLC. He summarizes the corporate and commercial decisions of Delaware Courts, as well as providing commentaries on legal ethics, at www.delawarelitigation.com.

ETHICS COLUMN
Francis G.X. Pileggi, Esquire

Supreme Court Denies In-house Counsel's Motion to Withdraw from *Pro Bono* Representation Due to Lack of Malpractice Insurance

The Delaware Supreme Court recently accepted two certified questions of law from the Delaware Family Court to address whether in-house counsel appointed to represent indigent parties could withdraw from court-appointed service due to lack of professional malpractice insurance coverage. The court also addressed the certified question regarding whether a court appointed attorney enjoys qualified immunity from malpractice liability. Delaware's high court ruled that the court appointed attorney, referred to in the opinion as Attorney X, did have qualified immunity from malpractice liability, but did not have sufficient cause to withdraw based on a lack of professional malpractice insurance coverage. *Hanson v. Morton*, No. 557, 2013 (Del. Supr., June 11, 2013).

Issue Presented

Pursuant to Delaware Supreme Court Rule 41, the Family Court certified two questions of law that the Delaware Supreme Court accepted: (1) Is an attorney serving as in-house counsel in corporate practice, who was appointed by Family Court to represent an indigent parent in pendency proceedings, provided with qualified immunity from malpractice liability in his or her role as court appointed counsel; (2) Whether or not such court appointed counsel is covered or is provided with qualified immunity, does the lack of malpractice insurance by in-house counsel constitute sufficient cause to withdraw from court appointed representation under Delaware Rule of Professional Conduct 6.2.

Procedural History

The case involved a petition for guardianship of a minor child. The Family Court appointed Attorney X, an in-house counsel at a large Delaware corporation, to represent the indigent parent.

Pursuant to its internal procedures, the Delaware Supreme Court assigned pseudonyms to the parties. The Mortons sought guardianship of a young child who was their nephew. The parents, the Hansons, also sought to be named as guardians. In light of their indigence, the Family Court appointed Attorney X to represent them. Attorney X is engaged in a corporate practice with a large corporation as in-house counsel and is not engaged in the private practice of law. Therefore, Attorney X is not obligated to certify in his annual registration statement with the Delaware Supreme Court that

he has insurance coverage for legal malpractice liability. Nor does his corporation maintain professional malpractice liability coverage for clients other than the corporation with whom he is employed. Based on the absence of such protection from exposure to potential malpractice claims, Attorney X moved to withdraw his representation on the ground that his appointment "poses an undue and unnecessary hardship."

Analysis

Regarding the question of qualified immunity, the court considered three potentially applicable Delaware statutes: the Good Samaritan Statute, the Office of Child Advocate Immunity Statute and the Tort Claims Act. The court determined that the only applicable statute was the Tort Claims Act.

The court examined the purpose of the Tort Claims Act, which is to: "discourage lawsuits which might create a chilling effect on the ability of public officials or employees to exercise their discretionary authority." *See* 16 *Del. C.* Section 6801(a). The Act applies to any public officer, whether elected or appointed if the person was acting in connection with an official duty, in good faith, and in the absence of gross or wanton negligence. The court described prior decisions in which the qualified immunity of the Tort Claims Act was determined to apply to public defenders as public employees of the state. In that prior decision, the court reasoned that public defenders would be entitled to qualified immunity under the Tort Claims Act but not absolute immunity. *See* 10 *Del. C.* Section 4010(1). In another prior decision, the Delaware Supreme Court had extended that same immunity to lawyers who were appointed by the court to represent indigent criminal defendants.

Delaware's high court reasoned that the same public policy considerations that support a qualified immunity for counsel appointed for indigent criminal defendants should apply to attorneys appointed to represent indigent parents in Family Court proceedings. Similar to attorneys appointed to represent indigent criminal defendants, those attorneys appointed to represent indigent parents have the same special relationship with their clients. Likewise, Family Court appointees do not have the ability to reject such clients or cases. Finally, attorneys appointed by the Family

Court promote the public welfare by "independently litigating claims of clients who might otherwise be left without representation."

Having concluded that the appointed Attorney X enjoyed qualified immunity, the court then turned to the issue of whether there was a sufficient basis to grant a motion to withdraw.

Delaware Rule of Professional Conduct 6.2 provides that a court-appointed attorney may only withdraw from the appointment for "good cause." Good cause includes when the representation will result in "an unreasonable financial burden on the lawyer." Additionally, DRPC 1.16(b)(6)-(7) allows an attorney to withdraw his or her representation "if it will result in an unreasonable financial burden or another good cause to withdraw exists."

The Delaware Supreme Court reasoned that the qualified immunity provided to the court appointed counsel based on Section 4001, Title 10 of the Delaware Code, does not support the argument that good cause exists for a court appointed attorney to withdraw from representation for lack of malpractice insurance. The court explained that no requirement to obtain insurance coverage is imposed by the court appointment. Moreover, the court reasoned that a malpractice claim will be subject to dismissal based upon the qualified immunity under the Torts Claims Act. Thus, the court concluded that any

financial burden would be *de minimis*. Therefore, the court held that Attorney X did not demonstrate sufficient good cause or an unreasonable financial burden that would support a motion to withdraw from the court appointed representation.

This decision provides helpful clarification for court appointed attorneys, whether in-house counsel or those in private practice, to the extent that their exposure to potential malpractice claims is minimized or non-existent based on a qualified immunity announced in this decision. One result of this opinion will be to provide some incentive for those who are willing to volunteer their services for those members of society that would otherwise not likely have the benefit of legal representation. Parenthetically, similar legal representation is provided by many civil rights groups to those who would otherwise not have legal representation. Those groups include one of the oldest civil rights groups in the United States, the National Rifle Association, as well as other groups such as the ACLU. Of course, the representation provided by those groups, however, does not enjoy qualified immunity. ◆

Francis G.X. Pileggi is the Member-in-Charge of the Wilmington, Delaware, office of Eckert Seamans Cherin & Mellott, LLC. He summarizes the corporate and commercial decisions of Delaware Courts, as well as providing commentaries on legal ethics, at www.delawarelitigation.com. He is a member of the Richard K. Herrmann AIC.

Advance Waiver Approved by Federal Court in Texas

An increasing number of law firms are asking clients to sign advance waivers that seek to minimize the risk of future disqualifications due to potential conflicts of interest, especially in the context of companies with many affiliates and large law firms with many offices. A recent federal court decision supported the enforceability of such advance waivers. In a decision of the United States District for the Northern District of Texas in *Galderma Labs, L.P. v. Actavis Mid Atl. LLC*, 2013 U.S. Dist. LEXIS 24171, the court concluded that Galderma gave informed consent to the representation by Vinson & Elkins of clients directly adverse to *Galderma* in substantially unrelated litigation and where there was no reasonable probability that confidential information would be used to Galderma's disadvantage. The court explained why the facts of this case supported that conclusion based on the application of four primary sources of authority: Comment 22 to Model Rule 1.7 of the ABA Rules of Professional Conduct, Comment 6 to Model Rule 1.0; ABA Formal Opinion 05-436; and §122 of the Restatement(Third) of the Law Governing Lawyers. The court distinguished the opinion in *Celgene Corp. v. KV Pharmaceutical Co.*, 2008 U.S. Dist. LEXIS 58735, in part because that decision did not give full effect to the 2002 amendments to the Model Rules, which recognize that under certain circumstances, general and open-ended consent to advance waivers of future conflicts may be valid.

Background

The *Galderma* case involved representation by V&E of Galderma Labs for employment related matters beginning in 2003. In 2012, while V&E was advising them on employment issues, the company filed an intellectual property lawsuit against Actavis which was also represented by V&E. Galderma Labs is a global company often represented by large law firms and also has an in-house legal department. Its affiliates have operations around the world and reported worldwide sales of approximately $1.8 billion in 2011.

The crux of the issue presented to the court was whether or not a sophisticated client, represented by in-house counsel, gave informed consent when it agreed to a general, open-ended waiver of future conflicts of interest in V&E's 2003 engagement letter.

The company argued that it did not give informed consent when it signed the agreement. By contrast, V&E argued that the waiver language was reasonably adequate to advise Galderma of the material risk of waiving future conflicts.

The exact language of the open-ended waiver of future conflicts involved in this case is critical to an understanding of the court's reasoning. The engagement letter signed by the client provided in part as follows:

> We understand and agree that this is not an exclusive agreement, and you are free to retain any other counsel of your choosing. We recognize that we shall be disqualified from representing any other client with interest materially and directly adverse to yours: (i) in any matter which is substantially related to our representation of you and (ii) with respect to any matter where there is a reasonable probability the confidential information you furnished to us could be used to your disadvantage. You understand and agree that, with those exceptions, we are free to represent other clients, including clients whose interest may conflict with ours in litigation, business transactions, or other legal matters. You agree that our representing you in this matter will not prevent or disqualify us from representing clients adverse to you in other matters and that you consent in advance to our undertaking such adverse representations.

Reasoning of the Court

The court recognized the potential for abuse when motions to disqualify are filed by opposing parties. The court also recognized that large law firms would never be able to take on small, specialized matters for a client unless those firms could reasonably protect against the potential abuse by preserving their ability to practice in other areas where the client has chosen to retain different counsel.

ABA Model Rule of Professional Conduct 1.7(b) acknowledges an exception to the general prohibition against a lawyer representing a client if their representation involves a concurrent conflict of interest. The exception applies if four criteria are satisfied: (1) the lawyer reasonably believes that the lawyer will be able to provide competent and diligent representation to each affected client; (2) the representation is not prohibited by law; (3) the representation does not involve the assertion of a claim by one client against another client represented by the lawyer in the same litigation or other proceeding before a tribunal; and (4) each affected client gives informed consent, confirmed in writing. (By comparison, the applicable Texas Rule does not require informed consent).

Much of the court's analysis addressed whether the consent provided in this case was informed consent. ABA Model Rule 1.0 defines informed consent as involving reasonable steps to ensure that the client or other person possesses information reasonably adequate to make an informed decision. *See* Rule 1.0, Cmt. 6. The three factors used to determine whether a disclosure is reasonably adequate to allow for informed consent pursuant to Rule 1.0 are first, whether the waiver identifies a course of conduct with regard to concurrent conflicts of interest. Second, whether the letter includes an explanation of the material risk of waiving future conflicts of interest. Third, the letter must explain an alternative course of conduct. The court found that an analysis of the facts of this case supported the conclusion that the company manifested informed consent.

Whether or not consent was informed turns on an objective standard of reasonable disclosure and reasonable understanding. An essential part of the analysis and reasoning of the Court was a determination that the company was a sophisticated client and that it had independent counsel when reviewing and agreeing to the advance waiver.

The waiver was reviewed by in-house counsel, regarded by the court as independent of Vinson & Elkins. Comment 6 to Rule 1.0 provides that "generally a client…who is independently represented by other counsel in giving their consent should be assumed to have given informed consent."

Conclusion

The court concluded that the company gave informed consent to V&E's representation of clients directly adverse to Galderma in substantially unrelated litigation. Because V&E's representation fell within the scope of that informed consent, V&E was not disqualified from representing Actavis.

This short ethics column cannot provide comprehensive treatment of the many nuances and factual details that are often determinative in these cases.

The concluding point that one should take away from this short overview is that advance waivers of potential future conflicts may be enforced by the courts if one carefully observes the applicable prerequisites controlling in one's jurisdiction. ◆

Francis G.X. Pileggi is the Member-in-Charge of the Wilmington, Delaware, office of Eckert Seamans Cherin & Mellott, LLC. He summarizes the corporate and commercial decisions of Delaware Courts, and provides commentaries on legal ethics, at www.delawarelitigation.com.

Second Circuit Disqualifies Attorney For Breach of Client Confidences

One of the fundamental principles that governs the relationship between an attorney and a client is that the attorney must maintain the confidence of information received from the client during the course of the representation. The U.S. Court of Appeals for the Second Circuit recently affirmed the disqualification of an in-house counsel who sued the corporation for whom he had previously served as general counsel. *U.S. v. Quest Diagnostics, Inc.*, No. 11-1565-cv (2nd Cir. Oct. 25, 2013).

Background

Briefly, the factual background involved a former general counsel who believed that the company that he worked for was overcharging the government for services performed for the government. He caused a *qui tam* action pursuant to the federal False Claims Act to be filed against his former company by a Delaware general partnership that he formed with the former CEO and former CFO. The three formed the entity for the purpose of filing the *qui tam* case. The reference to *qui tam* actions pursuant to the federal False Claims Act is a short reference for a longer Latin phrase that refers to a claim made by a private plaintiff on behalf of the government to recover a remedy for harm done to the government. A percentage of any recovery is awarded to the persons initiating the suit. The complete Latin phrase is *qui tam pro domino rege quam pro se ipso in hac parte sequitur,* which means "who pursues this action on our Lord the King's behalf as well as his own."

The general counsel ("the GC") involved in this case was the sole in-house lawyer for the defendant entity involved, during the relevant periods when the alleged fraudulent behavior involving the government took place. A noteworthy fact is that the general partnership formed by the GC and the former CEO and former CFO for purposes of filing the *qui tam* action could have been formed without the GC, and the *qui tam* action could have been pursued without the GC—with information known by the former CEO and the former CFO. However, the former CEO requested the involvement of the GC on the theory that it would lend more credibility to the *qui tam* action.

While working at the defendant company, the GC had expressed his concerns to the CEO at the time (who was not the same former CEO who was

part of the *qui tam* action), but the GC did not report his concerns to the full board. After the *qui tam* case was filed, the company filed a motion to dismiss and to disqualify the GC based on the argument that the GC violated New York Rule of Professional Conduct 1.9(a), sometimes known as the "side-switching rule," which generally prevents a lawyer who has formerly represented a client in a matter to thereafter represent another person in the same or a substantially related matter in which that person's interests are materially adverse to the interest of the former client, unless the former client gives informed consent, confirmed in writing. The GC argued that one of the exceptions, enumerated in Rule 1.6(b), permits a lawyer to reveal or use confidential information to the extent that the lawyer reasonably believes necessary to prevent the client from committing a crime.

The district court found that the GC had violated the ethical rule prohibiting the disclosure of client confidences, and the exception to the rule did not apply. The court also found the GC in violation of the "side-switching rule" embodied in Rule 1.9(a).

Appellate Ruling and Reasoning

The Second Circuit affirmed the trial court's finding that the GC violated the prohibition in Rule 1.9(c) in connection with disclosing client confidences that were used in the *qui tam* action against his former company, but the appellate court did not find it necessary to opine on the trial court's finding regarding the "side-switching rule".

The Second Circuit also upheld the remedy imposed by the district court for the violation, which was to dismiss the complaint and to disqualify not only the GC, but also the other two members of the general partnership formed to pursue the *qui tam* action. Counsel for the general partnership that served as the plaintiff in the *qui tam* action was also disqualified. The district court reasoned that those measures were necessary to protect the defendant company from the use of its confidential information against it.

The Second Circuit explained why the federal False Claims Act did not preempt state rules on legal ethics, notwithstanding the strong federal interests to encourage private individuals who are aware of fraud being perpetrated against the government to bring such information to light.

The Second Circuit agreed with the trial court that even though the GC could have believed that his former company had the intention to commit a crime and that his disclosure of client confidences was an exception permitted to prevent the commission of crime, the broad extent of the disclosures of client confidences by the GC went far beyond the information that was necessary in order to prevent the commission of a crime or to pursue the *qui tam* action. This was compounded by the lack of necessity for the GC to make any disclosures, which could have been made by the former CEO and the former CFO who were also pursuing the *qui tam* action through the general partnership that was formed to pursue the claims.

Prior Second Circuit decisions were cited in support of the position that trial judges have the power to disqualify attorneys where the attorney is "at least potentially in a position to use privileged information concerning the other side through prior representation." This power includes the dismissal of a complaint prepared in reliance on privileged information. The court also relied on prior decisions that support the disqualification of counsel for an attorney who has violated client confidences as in the instant case—even if counsel for the party did not commit any errors.

The court of appeals reasoned that even if counsel for the GC's partnership did not violate any ethical rules, the focus was on the prejudice to the former client whose confidences would be used against it. The Second Circuit reasoned that prior cases have found it necessary to dismiss counsel who had themselves committed no ethical violation on the basis that confidences could have been revealed to them that would prejudice a party in litigation. The appellate court noted in closing that compliance with legal ethics does not always involve morality or venality, but differences of opinion among honest men over the ethical propriety of conduct can still lead to the dismissal of counsel who did not violate those rules. ◆

Francis G.X. Pileggi, Esquire is the Member-in-Charge of the Wilmington, Delaware, office of Eckert Seamans Cherin & Mellott, LLC. He summarizes the corporate and commercial decisions of Delaware courts and provides commentary on legal ethics at www.delawarelitigation.com.

Federal Court Grants Motion to Disqualify Counsel Based on Rules 1.7, 1.9 and 1.10

In two separate cases, the U.S. District Court for the District of Delaware granted two separate motions in two separate cases to disqualify counsel based on the Model Rules of Professional Conduct. These decisions provide practical insights for practitioners confronted with issues that often arise when attorneys change firms and when it is not clear whether a prior client relationship had been terminated.

These cases are also noteworthy because prior decisions by the U.S. District Court for the District of Delaware have denied motions to disqualify based on different factual circumstances where attorneys in different offices of the same firm were arguably adverse to the same client. *See, e.g., Elonex I.P. Holdings v. Apple Computer, Inc.*, 142 F. Supp. 2d 579, 583 (D. Del. 2001). Also, by comparison, the Delaware Rules of Professional Conduct, which are slightly different than the Model Rules, are often applied by the Delaware state courts to disfavor disqualification even where a technical violation of the rule may exist, unless there is a material negative impact on the administration of justice. *See, e.g., In the matter of the Rehabilitation of Indemnity Insurance Corp.*, C.A. No. 8601-VCL (Del. Ch. Feb. 19, 2014).

In *Parallel Iron LLC v. Adobe Systems*, 2013 U.S. Dist. LEXIS 29382 (D. Del. 2013), the court addressed the claim that counsel for the plaintiff, Parallel Iron, served as opinion counsel for defendant Adobe at the time that Parallel Iron filed suit, thus creating an impermissible concurrent conflict of interest based on dual representation.

In this case the district court addressed the alleged breach of Model Rule 1.7(a) which prevents a lawyer from representing a client if the representation involves a concurring conflict of interest, absent client consent. Parallel Iron argued that there was no active attorney-client relationship at the time suit was filed. However, the court noted that under Delaware law even where no express contract or formal agreement evidencing an attorney-client relationship exists, courts look to the contacts between the potential client and its potential lawyer to determine whether it "would have been reasonable for the client to believe that the attorney was acting on its behalf as counsel." *See Boston Scientific Corp. v. Johnson & Johnson, Inc.*, 647 F. Supp. 2d 369, 373 (D. Del. 2009).

The court referred to Rule 1.16(b), which allows the termination of a client relationship by an attorney without any adverse impact on the client, but the burden is on the attorney to establish that termination. The court explained that even though no current work was either requested by the client or was being performed by the attorney, that alone would not suffice to establish the termination of the client relationship. The court relied on a New Jersey case for the position that a breach of Rule 1.7 seeks to protect the duty of loyalty, and a *"per se* rule of disqualification should be applied when that rule is breached." The court found that counsel in this case should have been more proactive to clarify and establish the termination of the relationship prior to filing suit.

In a separate case by the same court in the matter of *Enzo Life Sciences, Inc. v. Adipogen Corp.*, 2013 U.S. Dist. LEXIS 164939 (D. Del. 2013), the court addressed alleged infractions of Model Rules 1.9 and 1.10. This case involved lawyers who switched firms. A partner in the plaintiff's firm formerly was with the firm that represented the defendant. The court explained that the purpose of Rule 1.9(a) is to prevent the potential that a former client's confidence and secrets may be used against him.

The court also explained that Rule 1.10(a) provides that an attorney's conflicts are imputed to the firm at which he works unless certain requirements are met. The court recited the requirements under Rule 1.10(a)(2) that must be satisfied if the conflict arises from the work that an attorney performed at a prior firm. Those requirements include but are not limited to the creation of an ethical screen to prevent the participation of the attorney, and the court recited a list of many other factors that the courts consider in order to determine whether a screening is adequate.

After applying those multiple factors in this case, the court concluded that for several reasons the screen was not effective and the imputation of the conflict would require that the motion for disqualification be granted.

First, the court found that there was no prohibition that prevented the former defense counsel, who was now with the firm currently representing the plaintiff, from being in the presence of others in the firm who were discussing the case. Second, the screen provided no enforcement mechanism with penalties that would include termination for violation of the screen. The court found that a reminder e-mail informing employees of the firm that the screen must be followed was not sufficient nor was it tantamount to including in the original policy a penalty of termination for violation of the policy. In addition, the court was not persuaded that the former attorney for the defense firm would be able to satisfy Rule 1.10(a)(2)(i), which would prevent him from being apportioned any of the fee received by his new firm that represented the plaintiff. The court was influenced by the fact that the former attorney for the defendant's firm was now a named partner in the plaintiff's firm, and because of the relatively small size of the plaintiff's firm there was not sufficient evidence to demonstrate that the firm would be able to withhold any of the funds from this case to be shared with that attorney.

Lastly, the court explained that no actual prejudice is necessary in order for a motion to disqualify to be granted based on the public policy that clients must feel confident that they can divulge all relevant information to their attorneys without fear that such confidences will eventually be used against them in a later matter. Also important in the analysis of the court was a recitation of time entries that the attorney involved recorded on behalf of the defendant in the same litigation when he was previously a member of the firm currently representing the defendant.

These cases demonstrate the importance of addressing the factual nuances of potential conflicts when attorneys change firms, and to create clear documentation establishing when a client-relationship has been terminated. ◆

Francis G.X. Pileggi is the Member-in-Charge of the Wilmington, Delaware, office of Eckert Seamans Cherin & Mellott, LLC. He summarizes the corporate and commercial decisions of Delaware Courts, and provides commentaries on legal ethics, at www.delawarelitigation.com.

New Lateral Partner Creates Conflict that Disqualifies His New Firm

This month's ethics column will be a short overview of the Philadelphia Bar Association's Professional Ethics Committee Opinion 2014-1 (April 2014), relating to the conflict issues that arise when a lateral partner joins a law firm. The facts on which Opinion 2014-1 is based include a law firm partner ("Partner") who was representing a criminal defendant in a securities fraud case ("Client"). A new lateral recently joined the Partner's firm ("Lateral").

Prior to joining the firm, Lateral had acted as counsel for the primary government witness against Client, and negotiated a plea deal for the witness in return for cooperation with the U.S. Attorney including an agreement to testify against Client. Lateral no longer represents the witness.

Partner anticipates that he will need to vigorously cross-examine the witness that Lateral formerly represented, in order for Partner to represent Client effectively. Neither Lateral nor Partner would advise their respective clients to waive any potential conflicts, but in any event they asked the Professional Ethics Committee for its opinion on whether there was a non-waivable conflict. It was not disputed that Client and the witness that Lateral formerly represented were adverse to each other in the same litigation. *See, e.g., United States v. Moses*, 58 Fed. App. 549, 552 (3rd Cir. 2003).

Rule 1.6 (c)(7) of the Pennsylvania Rules of Professional Conduct was the first rule considered by the Committee, and that rule pertaining to confidentiality of information, provides that:

> (c) A lawyer may reveal such information to the extent that the lawyer reasonably believes necessary:
>
> …
>
> (7) to detect and resolve conflicts of interest from the lawyer's change of employment or from changes in the composition or ownership of a firm, but only if the revealed information would not compromise the attorney-client privilege or otherwise prejudice the client.

The Committee next considered Rule 1.7 relating to conflicts of interest with current clients, and that rule provides in relevant part that:

> (a) Except as provided in paragraph (b), a lawyer shall not represent a client if the

representation involves a concurrent conflict of interest. A concurrent conflict of interest exists if:

> (1) the representation of one client will be directly adverse to another client;

or

> (2) there is a significant risk that the representation of one or more clients will be materially limited by the lawyer's representation of another client, a former client or a third person, or by a personal interest of the lawyer. (emphasis added).

Rule 1.9, entitled "Duties to Former Clients," was next examined. Rule 1.9 provides that:

> (a) A lawyer who has formally represented a client in a matter shall not thereafter represent another person in the same or a substantially related matter in which that person's interests are materially adverse to the interest of the former client unless the former client gives informed consent.

> (b) A lawyer shall not knowingly represent a person in the same or a substantially related matter in which a firm with which the lawyer formerly was associated had previously represented a client

> (1) whose interests are materially adverse to that person; and

> (2) about whom the lawyer had acquired information protected by Rules 1.6 and 1.9 (c) that is material to the matter;

> unless the former client gives informed consent.

> (c) A lawyer who has formerly represented a client in a matter or whose present or former firm has formerly presented a client in a matter shall not thereafter:

> (1) use information relating to the representation to the disadvantage of the former client except as these Rules would permit or require with respect to a client, or when the information has become generally known; and

(2) reveal information relating to the representation except as these Rules would permit or require with respect to a client.

The last rule considered by the committee was Rule 1.10, entitled "Imputation of Conflicts of Interest: General Rule," which provides that:

(a) While lawyers are associated with a firm, none of them shall knowingly represent a client when one of them practicing alone would be prohibited from doing so by Rules 1.7 or 1.9, unless the prohibition is based on a personal interest of the prohibited lawyer and does not represent a significant risk of materially limiting the representation of the client by the remaining lawyers in the firm, or unless permitted by Rules 1.10 (b) or (c).

(b) When a lawyer becomes associated with a firm, the firm may not knowingly represent a person in the same or a substantially related matter in which that lawyer, or a firm with which the lawyer was associated, had previously represented a client whose interests are materially adverse to that person and about whom the lawyer had acquired information protected by Rules 1.6 and 1.9 (c) that is material to the matter unless:

(1) the disqualified lawyer is screened from any participation in the matter and is apportioned no part of the fee therefrom; and

(2) written notice is promptly given to the appropriate client to enable it to ascertain compliance with the provisions of this rule.

The Committee concluded that Lateral carried with him a conflict that disqualified Partner and the new firm. This result may have been avoided if Lateral was screened from any participation in the matter that Partner was handling. The Committee found that Lateral was not screened as contemplated by Rule 1.10 (b)(1) and appropriate notice was not provided pursuant to Rule 1.10 (b)(2), and thus his disqualification was imputed to Partner and the whole new firm that Lateral joined. A more rigorous vetting of this conflict prior to Lateral starting at the new firm may have led to a different conclusion. In light of information already shared, establishing a screen at this point would be ineffective.

As a consequence of this Opinion, the committee advised that Partner could no longer represent Client, nor could Lateral resume representation of his former client if requested to do so. The committee noted that for future guidance it recommended reliance on Rule 1.6(c)(7) which allows disclosure of client information to the extent it is only being used to do a conflicts check for potential lateral candidates who are joining a new firm. This would also permit the implementation of an ethical screen that would eliminate the inadvertent exchange of confidential information between counsel for potentially adverse clients or former clients.

Of course, the rules of professional conduct vary from state to state, but the basic principles are typically shared, and the cautionary tale included in this opinion has relevance far beyond the boundaries of Pennsylvania. Those who are involved in the hiring of lateral lawyers should be aware of the issues raised in this opinion and be prepared to avoid the unhappy result visited upon the lawyers described in this short column. ◆

Francis G.X. Pileggi is the Member-in-Charge of the Wilmington, Delaware, office of Eckert Seamans Cherin & Mellott, LLC. His e-mail address is fpileggi@eckertseamans.com. He summarizes corporate and commercial decisions of Delaware courts and addresses issues of legal ethics at www.delawarelitigation.com.

ETHICS COLUMN
Francis G.X. Pileggi, Esquire

Delaware Court of Chancery Enforces Deposition Practice Standards

This latest ethics column will provide an overview of the highlights from a recent decision by the Delaware Court of Chancery in which deposition practice standards were described and enforced. In general, reading court decisions regarding the enforcement of discovery practice standards are akin to passing a car accident on the road and thinking: "there, but for the grace of God, go I." Nonetheless, those who toil in the vineyards of litigation practice infrequently find court decisions that clearly articulate the applicable standards and also enforce those standards with equal clarity. The reason that there are so few such decisions are manifold. One reason is that it remains expensive and time-consuming to engage in motion practice, and motion practice on discovery disputes and the result of the effort are often unsatisfying when courts take an approach of "a pox on both your houses," and pay no heed to which party started the imbroglio.

Recently in the matter of *In re: Appraisal of Dole Food Company, Inc.*, (Del. Ch. Dec. 9, 2014), the Delaware Court of Chancery interpreted its own Rule 37 to require fee-shifting based on an improper instruction to a deponent that the deponent should refuse to answer a question during the deposition, based merely on an argument that the question was either irrelevant or not likely to lead to the introduction of admissible evidence. The Delaware Rules of Civil Procedure are based on the Federal Rules of Civil Procedure.

The law in Delaware has been clear that during a deposition it is improper for a lawyer to instruct the deponent not to answer a question. Very limited exceptions apply, such as to protect an attorney/client privilege or to allow time for the filing of a motion to seek a protective order. Neither exception applied in this case.

The larger factual issue involved an effort to obtain valuations that the plaintiff had prepared prior to the litigation, which began in the form of a request for documents. After that request was rejected, the defendant company then noticed a deposition for a Rule 30(b)(6) witness. During the deposition similar questions were asked about the prior valuations, but the deponent was instructed not to answer questions regarding prior valuations based on an objection that the questions lacked relevance.

Dole moved to compel production of the valuation-related documents and for a supplemental deposi-

tion of the Rule 30(b)(6) witness. The 35-page decision of the court provided an extensive factual background of the dispute. For purposes of widespread applicability, I will focus on aspects of the opinion useful for every lawyer who tries to maintain civility and productivity in depositions.

Permissible Discovery
The court began its analysis with a review of the broad scope of permissible discovery pursuant to Rule 26(b)(1), which essentially allows discovery regarding any matter that is not privileged. It is not grounds for objection that the information will not be admissible at trial as long as the information sought "appears reasonably calculated to lead to the discovery of admissible evidence."

Nonetheless, objections to discovery in this case were made on the grounds of relevance, although the plaintiff abandoned that position in response to the motion to compel. The court explained that, in any event, the valuation materials prepared prior to the lawsuit may lead to admissible evidence. Prior Chancery decisions have so held.

The court explained that under Rule 26(b)(1), the burden to demonstrate that the discovery sought is reasonably calculated to lead to the introduction of admissible evidence is a slight burden, but after that minimal explanation is provided by the requesting party, it is the burden of the party opposing discovery to show that the explanation provided is erroneous and that the Rule 26(b)(1) standard has not been met. The Delaware decisions are consistent with federal decisions on this point.

The court also provided an explanation of those instances where the communication of an in-house lawyer is not an attorney/client privileged communication because that in-house attorney was providing business advice as opposed to legal advice. In those instances where it is a close call, as here, for one small portion of the discovery requested, the court conducted an in camera review. That was but a small aspect of the dispute, however, in this case.

Mandatory Fee-Shifting
The court interpreted Court of Chancery Rule 37(b)(2) to require mandatory fee-shifting when a party is "found to have failed to honor a discovery

request unless the court finds that the failure was substantially justified or that other circumstances make an award of expenses unjust." In this case, the court did not find the failure to be substantially justified nor did it find other circumstances that would make an award of expenses unjust. The primary reasoning of the court was that the objection to the production of documents and the instruction to a deponent not to answer a question based on relevance justified fee-shifting. That objection to potential admissibility was also contrary to prior precedent in appraisal actions. The court instructed that the proper procedure that should have been followed would have been for the attorney for the deponent to seek a motion for protective order to the extent that the petitioner believed that prior precedent should be distinguished or applied to reach a different result, in support of the non-discoverability of the inquiry.

Rule 30(c) provides that "evidence objected to [during a deposition] shall be taken subject to the objection." The deposition rules prevent an attorney from instructing a witness not to answer deposition questions based on relevance. Rather, "instructions not to answer only would be permissible on grounds of privilege or to enforce a limitation on evidence directed by the court."

In sum, the court awarded reasonable costs, including fees, incurred in taking the aborted Rule 30(b)(6) depositions and in bringing the motion to compel. The court explained that this award was not the same as penalty for bad faith litigation conduct. Rather, it was "simply the consequence contemplated by Rule 37 as part of an incentive structure intended by the drafters of the amended rule to limit the need for judicial intervention in discovery disputes." ◆

Francis G.X. Pileggi is the member-in-charge of the Wilmington, Delaware, office of Eckert Seamans Cherin & Mellott, LLC. He summarizes key corporate and commercial decisions of Delaware's Supreme Court and Court of Chancery at www.delawarelitigation.com.

Professionalism and Judges

For the last 15 years or so that I have written this column on legal ethics, I have focused primarily on the standards that lawyers are expected to follow as well as court decisions where those standards have been applied. By comparison, much less legal literature exists regarding the standards that judges should follow and many fewer court opinions exist where standards that judges are expected to follow have been enforced. Is less written about the unprofessional behavior of judges because it does not exist or because it is proportionately less of a problem?

The standard of conduct that we should expect from judges is rarely the subject of articles for various reasons including the obvious: reluctance to offend the jurists before whom one might make his or her living. In addition, the various codes of judicial conduct are typically enforced by other judges.

The theme of this issue of *The Bencher* is professionalism. The focus of this article will be a happy and positive one. This column will describe a few highlights of the induction ceremony for one of the newest members of the federal judiciary, Judge Mark A. Kearney. Based on his background and character as demonstrated through many years of practice, I predict that he will set the standard of judicial behavior by which others will be measured.

By describing the background and character of a new federal judge, my intent is to suggest that the past comportment of a person who is elevated to the bench is a helpful indicator of the future behavior of that judge while serving on the bench. When we hear stories about, or read opinions from, judges who are unnecessarily harsh in their rejection of an argument or unnecessarily belittling of lawyers who appear before them, one might inquire: did the judge treat others that way before ascending to the bench? How those jurists treated others who angered them or disagreed with them before donning the black robe is a helpful indicator of the performance of those same persons after they join of the ranks of the judiciary.

At the induction ceremony of Kearney as the newest judge of the U.S. District Court for the Eastern District of Pennsylvania, much of the program included testimonials by colleagues, friends and other judges about the type of person Kearney is, and has been. Many of the speakers at the ceremony indicated that during his many years of practice, they could not remember Kearney yelling in anger or deriding colleagues or others that he interacted with either on the job or on a personal level. A common theme in their description of the new judicial officer was that he is someone who is always jovial and quick to laugh. That assessment is consistent with my experience when I first met him during the year he served as a law clerk for the Delaware Court of Chancery. It would be hard to imagine this new judge treating anyone with less than complete respect, whether in his written opinions or on the bench. He joked with his new colleagues during his induction, that his experience in the Court of Chancery taught him how handling expedited cases can be part of routine daily procedures for a trial judge.

After his service as a judicial law clerk in Delaware, he joined the firm of Elliott, Greenleaf & Siedzikowski where he became a managing shareholder, with offices in Delaware and Pennsylvania. As a member of the Delaware and Pennsylvania Bars he accumulated many honors and much professional recognition in connection with his national trial practice that focused on commercial, class, derivative and financial litigation. He is a prolific writer. For example, he was a lead author of two volumes of the *Villanova Law Review* on Delaware fiduciary standards, and has written over twenty scholarly articles on commercial and corporate litigation.

Kearney serves as the current president of the Pennsylvania Bar Institute and was the president of the Montgomery Bar Association. He has represented dozens of abused children in criminal and dependency trials through the Montgomery Child Advocacy Project, and was a long-time director of Legal Aid of Southeastern Pennsylvania. He was also an appointed member of the Lawyers' Advisory Committee for the U.S. Court of Appeals for the Third Circuit.

In his remarks, and in the presentations by others about him, an often repeated refrain was that Kearney truly cares about people, and believes that all deserve to be treated with dignity regardless of their station in life. His wife and two children are his highest priorities, but other relatives and a large group of friends and colleagues are counted among his extended family. His Catholic faith and Irish heritage are key parts to understanding this newest jurist. For example, for many years he attended an annual Catholic weekend retreat with his father, and the Gaelic word for family was featured prominently throughout his acceptance speech.

In his remarks after he took the oath of office, Kearney described how his parents instilled in him the values of hard work, humility, concern for others, perseverance, and integrity. He worked his way through law school at a grocery store, which undoubtedly gave him an appreciation for the challenges of the blue collar work force. One of the other common themes in the description by others of Kearney was his friendly demeanor, and his ability to bring people together to "get a job done—and quickly."

These highlights of the background and character of Kearney promise that his judicial tenure will be marked by professionalism and high standards of judicial conduct that the best judges exemplify. Consistent with his reputation and the description of his character by those who have worked with him, one would not expect Kearney to belittle or be condescending to the attorneys appearing before him.

Articles about professionalism more often than not emphasize how lawyers should behave. Professionalism also must be expected of the judiciary, and it remains equally important for judges to treat lawyers and others who appear before them with the same respect, courtesy, and dignity that all lawyers should exhibit, both orally and in writing.

Kearney's life has exhibited the hallmarks of professionalism to which lawyers and judges alike should aspire. Based on that track record, I have every confidence that Judge Kearney's tenure on the federal bench will be a paradigm for the highest standards of judicial conduct. ◆

Francis G.X. Pileggi is the member-in-charge of the Wilmington, Delaware, office of Eckert Seamans Cherin & Mellott, LLC. His e-mail address is fpileggi@eckertseamans.com. He summarizes key corporate and commercial decisions of Delaware's Supreme Court and Court of Chancery at www.delawarelitigation.com.

Judge Criticized for Courtroom Behavior

The Michigan Supreme Court recently issued an opinion that describes courtroom behavior by a trial judge that warranted the reversal of a conviction. The case involved the conviction of a father for the death of his young child.

The Michigan Supreme Court determined that the trial judge's conduct deprived the defendant of a fair trial by piercing the veil of judicial impartiality. The court determined that the conduct of a judge pierces this veil and violates the constitutional guarantee of a fair trial when, "considering the totality of the circumstances, it is reasonably likely that the judge's conduct improperly influenced the jury by creating the appearance of advocacy or partiality against the party."

In this case, styled as *People v. Stevens*, the Michigan Supreme Court developed a five-part test for determining when the conduct of a trial judge pierced the veil of judicial impartiality. The five-part test includes: (1) nature of the judicial intervention; (2) tone and demeanor of the judge; (3) scope of the conduct in light of the trial's complexity; (4) whether the intervention was directed toward a particular party, so as to distinguish excessive but ultimately neutral questioning from biased judicial questioning; and (5) curative instructions at the close of a trial.

Application of the Standards to the Facts
Nature of Judicial Intervention

As applied to the facts of this case, Michigan's highest appellate court found that the trial judge undermined the testimony of the key expert witness for the defendant by suggesting that another witness offered contradictory testimony. The trial judge also contrasted the defense expert's opinion with the opinion of others and undermined the credibility of the defendant's expert. Specific examples were provided in the opinion of questioning by the trial judge that exceeded the bounds of permissive judicial conduct to the extent that it created an appearance of advocacy or partiality against the defendant.

Tone and Demeanor

This factor often dovetails with an analysis of the nature and type of judicial conduct. In this case, the trial judge's questioning of the expert for the defendant indicated antagonism and hostility.

For example, in one instance the judge asked three questions in immediate succession without giving the witness the chance to respond. At other points, the trial judge displayed hostility towards defense counsel and also expressed his personal opinion, doubting the testimony of the defendant. Although the actual tone and demeanor may not be expressed in the trial transcript, it can be inferred from the judge's choice of words, and in this instance the Michigan Supreme Court concluded that the trial judge created an appearance of bias against the defendant.

Scope of the Conduct in Light of the Trial's Complexity

Although this case involved an eight-day murder trial involving testimony from several medical experts, the level of complexity of the issues did not warrant the extent of the judicial intervention that occurred. The supreme court determined that counsel for both parties developed the differing viewpoints of the experts in an understandable fashion and that the degree of intervention by the trial judge was not justified.

Direction of Intervention Towards a Particular Party

The record of the trial indicated that the questioning of the trial judge was directed against the defendant and in favor of the prosecution. For example, it appeared that almost all the questions were directed toward defense witnesses. Even when the judge did ask questions of a prosecution witness, the inquiry often appeared to be intended to weaken the defendant's case. In contrast to the aggressive and undermining judicial examination of the defendant and the defense witness, no witness of the other side was subjected to such hostile intervention, according to the supreme court's analysis.

Curative Instructions

Although the trial judge gave a curative instruction that his intervention was not meant to reflect a personal opinion, and that his comments and questions were not evidence, based on a totality of the circumstances, this element of the test did not outweigh the other factors considered.

Conclusion

Based on application of all the factors to the facts of this case, the Michigan Supreme Court determined that the record reflected that the trial judge exhibited bias against the defense through-out the trial and, therefore, the case was remanded for a new trial before a different judge.

Commentary

The Court used the expression "piercing the veil of judicial impartiality" to describe the net effect when the trial judge gave the appearance of advocacy or partiality against a party, thereby depriving a party of a fair trial. The five-part test applied is equally applicable to civil trials. The Michigan Supreme Court did not discuss how those standards would apply in a bench trial, but there is reason to believe that most of the standards would apply as well, to the extent that the statements of a trial judge may demonstrate a lack of impartiality.

Experienced practitioners know that it remains rare to have a sufficient basis in the record as overwhelming as the evidence was in this case to challenge a judge's courtroom behavior. More often than not, if there is any questionable conduct, it is not sufficient to rise to the level that supported the result in the case highlighted in this short column. Judges are not perfect and measurements of trial conduct lacks mathematical precision. Therefore, a formulaic approach is not realistic when evaluating whether subtle or not so subtle comments or other actions by a trial judge during trial indicate a trial judge's predilection for the position of one party or the other. Of course, in a bench trial when the judge also serves as the fact finder, there are different considerations beyond those that would otherwise be present in a jury trial.

Nonetheless, decisions similar to the Michigan Supreme Court ruling in this case are rare because trial judges seldom provide the basis for reversal that existed in this decision. ◆

Francis G.X. Pileggi is the member-in-charge of the Wilmington, Delaware, office of Eckert Seamans Cherin & Mellott, LLC. His e-mail address is fpileggi@eckertseamans.com. He summarizes the key corporate and commercial decisions of Delaware Courts at www.delawarelitigation.com.

Prosecutorial Discretion

Over the many years that I have written this ethics column, the topics have mostly focused on court decisions applying the rules of professional conduct and other standards governing lawyers. This time, I review a ruling that addresses the concept of prosecutorial discretion.

This short article will highlight the key facts and issues published in a recent California ruling that dismissed charges against a lawyer who endured a trial based on an accusation that she failed to maintain client funds in a trust account. The post-trial decision was issued by a judge of the State Bar Court of California in the matter of Dianna Lynne Albini.

The court's opinion reviewed the evidence presented at a three-day trial. The Office of Chief Trial Counsel of the State Bar of California (State Bar) filed charges against respondent in November 2014. The trial was held in September 2015. Respondent was admitted to practice law in California in 1991. In 2007, she settled a personal injury matter. She withheld $50,000 in escrow in order to cover a lien for medical bills. After she closed her law practice, she was appointed as an administrative law judge in 2009. Apparently, California law only required her to keep her records for five years, after which time she discarded them. Her custom was to send letters to clients to give them notice prior to discarding their files. There is a factual dispute in this matter whether or not that notice was sent or received, and whether the medical bills were paid from respondent's escrow account.

In 2014, after reviewing her files in the case, the client for whom the respondent settled the personal injury matter, sent a letter to the respondent asking about the status of the $50,000 held in escrow. By that time, the respondent's law practice was closed and the respondent was an administrative law judge.

The trial revealed that the prosecutor's investigator contacted the potential lienholder and was told that there was no indication in their records of any collection efforts to collect any outstanding amounts from the client. If there were an unpaid amount or a lien, there would be an indication of collection efforts, but there were none. As far as the potential lienholder was concerned, the amount that would have been the subject of a lien, should be considered as paid in full. Likewise, it should be emphasized that neither a lien was asserted nor was the former client asked to pay the amount that one could presume was paid from the sum withheld in the respondent's trust account.

In addition, the respondent testified at trial that her recollection was that she paid the medical provider the full amount of $50,000 to satisfy and settle the slighter higher amount of medical bills for which payment was due at the time of the personal injury settlement. The State Bar had no contrary evidence that rose to the level of clear and convincing, which was the standard the prosecution had to meet at trial. The State Bar knew that it lacked such evidence prior to trial.

The records from the bank where the respondent's trust account was held were not complete. Nonetheless, the bank records that did exist demonstrated that during the relevant time period amounts equal to the sum withheld for the potential lien were paid to a third-party other than the respondent.

Respondent was charged with misappropriating client funds, which in this case, in California is a felony that, among other penalties, can lead to disbarment. The trial judge found that the State Bar did not introduce any affirmative evidence that respondent misappropriated funds. The court's opinion concluded that: "Considering this lack of proof and the documentary evidence that the charges had been paid…," there was no clear and convincing evidence to find respondent culpable of misappropriation of funds. Likewise, the trial judge found that there was insufficient evidence that respondent failed to maintain properly the appropriate client funds in her trust account. Therefore, the court dismissed with prejudice the two counts of professional misconduct.

In the meantime, respondent was removed from her position as an administrative judge. And where does she go to regain her tarnished reputation? ◆

Francis G.X. Pileggi, Esquire, is the member-in-charge of the Wilmington, Delaware, office of Eckert Seamans Cherin & Mellott, LLC. He summarizes the key corporate and commercial decisions of Delaware Courts at www.delawarelitigation.com.

Court Disqualifies Firm Based on Representation of Affiliated Subsidiary

This ethics column provides highlights of a recent decision in which the court disqualified a law firm based on a conflict of interest that arose in connection with the law firm's representation of two subsidiaries. In the case styled *Atlantic Specialty Insurance Company v. Premera Blue Cross*, 2016 WL 1615430 (W.D. Wash. April 22, 2016), the court was presented with a motion to disqualify the law firm representing Premera ("Law Firm") based on the concurrent representation by the Law Firm of an affiliate of the plaintiff, Atlantic, in a separate and unrelated matter. In this insurance coverage dispute, Atlantic sought a declaration that it had no duty to defend Premera under the policy issued by Atlantic regarding an underlying class action suit filed against Premera.

Atlantic's corporate structure is key to understanding the court's decision. Atlantic is a wholly-owned subsidiary of OneBeacon Insurance Group ("Parent"). Homeland Insurance Company of New York ("Homeland") is also a wholly-owned subsidiary of Parent. Both Atlantic and Homeland share the same mailing address and principle place of business as Parent. Both subsidiaries also share claims-handling services that are managed by the same claims unit personnel.

In July 2015, Parent received a claim on a policy issued by Homeland to AAM, Inc. Law Firm was hired to represent Homeland in a coverage dispute with AAM. In December 2015, Atlantic initiated the instant litigation against Premera, seeking a declaratory judgment that it had no duty to defend Premera under the policy that was issued to it by Atlantic. Law Firm had been representing Premera in the underlying litigation and entered its appearance on behalf of Premera in the declaratory judgment action.

In-house counsel for Atlantic notified Law Firm that there was a conflict of interest because Law Firm represented Atlantic's sister subsidiary, Homeland, in the AAM matter. Thus, Atlantic took the position that there was a conflict of interest because Atlantic and Homeland, as subsidiaries of Parent, consider themselves one client. They did not consent to the Law Firm being adverse to them in the instant case. The Law Firm refused to withdraw and a motion to disqualify was filed. Law Firm's position was that Atlantic and Homeland are two distinct corporations and should not be considered one client for purposes of an analysis of conflicts of interest. The court disagreed with that position.

After this issue arose, the Law Firm withdrew its representation of Homeland and argued that the appropriate analysis at that point was based on the rule that applies to conflicts with former clients. The court applied Rule 1.7 of the State of Washington's Rules of Professional Conduct, which applies to conflicts with current clients. The representation of Homeland was concurrent with the representation adverse to Atlantic. The Law Firm's subsequent termination of representation of Homeland did not make the rule for former clients applicable. Sometimes referred to as the "hot potato" rule, the policy supporting the avoidance of conflicts would be subverted if firing one client, after a conflict arose, would allow the more lenient Rule 1.9 to apply.

The more stringent rule relating to current conflicts, Rule 1.7, provides that unless certain requirements are met, "a lawyer shall not represent a client if the representation involves a concurrent conflict of interest. A concurrent conflict of interest exists if: (1) the representation of one client would be directly adverse to another client; or (2) there is a significant risk that the representation of one or more clients will be materially limited by the lawyer's responsibility to another client, a former client or a third person or by a personal interest of the lawyer."

Rule 1.9 applies to the duties of a lawyer to former clients and provides that: "A lawyer who has formerly represented a client in a matter shall not thereafter represent another person in the same or a substantially related matter in which that person's interests are materially adverse to the interests of the former client unless the former client gives informed consent, confirmed in writing." Comment 3 to Rule 1.9 provides that "matters are 'substantially related' for purposes of this Rule if they involve the same transaction or legal dispute or there otherwise is a substantial risk that confidential factual information as would normally have been obtained in the prior representation would materially advance the client's position in the subsequent matter."

Rule 1.7 is less forgiving than Rule 1.9 and disqualifies an attorney from concurrently representing two

Ethics *continued from page 11.*

clients with adverse interests, even if the matters are wholly unrelated. The court reasoned that the two subsidiaries involved in this matter should be treated as one client for purposes of a conflicts analysis. They share the same mailing address and principle place of business. Both entities are structured so that their claims-handling services are managed by the same personnel. The same employees handle all insurance coverage litigation commenced by or against Atlantic and Homeland. The same claims attorney involved in this instant matter with Premera was also the claims attorney handling the AAM matter with Homeland.

The court was not persuaded by the Law Firm's argument that it was not aware of the relationship between Atlantic and Homeland, and was previously adverse to Atlantic. The court explained that attorneys are responsible for knowing the relationship between or among related corporate clients, and the duty is imposed on the attorney— not the client—to be familiar with the affiliates and related companies of a client. Even though the Law Firm did not consider itself as having an attorney-client relationship with the other subsidiary, the court instructed that the existence of an attorney-client relationship is determined based on the reasonable understanding of the client, not the view of the attorney. Even though the Law Firm did not know that Atlantic and Homeland were both subsidiaries of the Parent, the court found that they should have known.

The court was mindful that disqualification of counsel is a drastic measure as it impacts a client's right to choose counsel and can be disruptive to the litigation process, especially as in this case where the attorney-client relationship spanned nearly two decades.

The court reasoned that one of the policies behind the rule was to avoid an "appearance of an impropriety" and the termination of one client to avoid the application of Rule 1.7 was contrary to that policy. The court added that some cases have found that, even if there is no strict contractual attorney-client relationship that would support an application of Rule 1.7, "fiduciary obligations and professional responsibilities may warrant disqualification of counsel in appropriate cases…." *See Unified Sewage Agency of Washington County, Or. v. Jelco Inc.*, 646 F.2d 1339, 1345 n.4 (9th Cir. 1981). ◆

Francis G.X. Pileggi, Esquire, is the member-in-charge of the Wilmington, Delaware, office of Eckert Seamans Cherin & Mellott, LLC. He summarizes the key corporate and commercial decisions of Delaware Courts at www.delawarelitigation.com.

ABA Seeks to Enforce Political Correctness

During the nearly two decades that I have written this ethics column, I have eschewed controversial topics. Not this time.

In August, the American Bar Association adopted a new Model Rule of Professional Conduct 8.4(g), which creates a new definition for discrimination against certain protected classes. The Model Rules approved by the ABA are typically adopted by each state at which time a violation of any rule could subject a lawyer to penalties that include disbarment or suspension from the practice of law.

It is a violation of the new Rule 8.4(g) to engage in discrimination based on "race, sex, religion, national origin, ethnicity, disability, age, sexual orientation, gender identity, marital status, or socioeconomic status in conduct related to the practice of law." Discrimination includes "verbal" conduct that "manifests bias."

One leading expert on constitutional law and legal ethics, Professor Ronald Rotunda, has written recently in *The Wall Street Journal* that the new rule is in conflict with the First Amendment right to free speech. He uses the example of two lawyers discussing a case and one exclaims: "I abhor the idle rich. We should raise capital gains taxes." According to the good professor, that lawyer has just violated the new ABA rule "by manifesting bias based on socioeconomic status."

Another example could involve a law firm that rejects a young man's application for a job as a messenger. If the law firm designates their restrooms by sex, the applicant could argue that the firm engaged in "gender identity" discrimination. If the disgruntled messenger identifies with the opposite sex (or says that he does), he could assert that he was not hired because the firm demonstrated gender-identity bias based on the firm's restrooms being segregated.

Another widely-respected constitutional law scholar, Professor Eugene Volokh, has written that state courts and state bars should resist pressure to adopt the new rule. Volokh explains that the new rule could even expose a solo practitioner to penalties if something she "said at a law-related function offended someone employed by some other law firm."

Moreover, in his expert view, the rule does nothing to limit the rule's impact on the First Amendment right to free speech. He adds that the ABA intends to: "limit lawyers' expression of viewpoints that it disapproves of."

The ABA's membership includes less than one-third of the approximately 1.2 million lawyers in the United States. Another highly-regarded legal scholar, often cited in court opinions, Professor Stephen Bainbridge, has written on his blog, in connection with the new rule, that the "ABA no longer represents the interests of all lawyers but only those who belong to the PC crowd."

Another lawyer who frequently publishes articles on the right to free speech has written about the new rule to argue that he could be subject to professional penalties for publicly expressing his view that same-sex marriage is contrary to religious principles to which he adheres. He expresses concern that, as with other speech codes, the chilling effect resulting from fear of enforcement remains at least as problematic as actual enforcement. The chilling effect will create the impression that certain ideas that are not politically correct, and that could be perceived as offensive by certain favored victim groups, are verboten. Will the new rule subject lawyers to the expense of defending ethics complaints if a conversation over a drink at a bar association event is now within the jurisdiction of the thought police? Even if no ethics complaint is filed, will someone who is expressing religious beliefs that are not politically correct, be verbally tarred and feathered as "one of those people"— bigots and haters? Will law firms need to change the signs for all restrooms used by their employees to label them all as gender-neutral restrooms?

Even if the newly unethical speech does not violate state or federal law, it could still be a violation of the new rule. The new restrictions on what lawyers are allowed to say may ameliorate unemployment, especially among young lawyers who might consider specializing in this new area.

It remains to be seen how vigorous the enforcement will be of the new orthodoxy against those committing the sin of political incorrectness in its latest iteration? ◆

Francis G.X. Pileggi is the member-in-charge of the Wilmington, Delaware, office of Eckert Seamans Cherin & Mellott, LLC. He summarizes key corporate and commercial decisions of Delaware Courts, and addresses legal ethics, at www.delawarelitigation.com.

Delaware Imposes Penalties for Litigation Misconduct

The Delaware Supreme Court recently upheld a decision of the Delaware Court of Chancery imposing a penalty of more than $7 million in legal fees incurred by the opposing party in connection with a business dispute between two co-owners of a successful company. The fee-shifting was based on a finding of litigation misconduct. This opinion serves as a useful reminder for all litigants that at least in one state failure of the parties to comply with important standards of litigation conduct will be met with serious penalties.

The formal written opinions on various aspects of this case by the Court of Chancery and Supreme Court combined exceed 200-pages, along with footnotes of a greater number. This article highlights the decision regarding actions that supported the fee shifting as a penalty. In connection with the hotly contested, complex litigation, both parties claimed breaches of fiduciary duty, and sought the court's help to break a deadlock among the co-owners of a company that generated annual revenue of over $500 million. The court found after an evidentiary hearing that one of the parties: (1) deleted documents from his laptop, even after litigation-hold notices were circulated, and after an order from the court requiring the production of the laptop; (2) recklessly failed to safeguard information on a cell phone; (3) improperly gained access to the emails of another party in the litigation; and (4) lied multiple times in response to discovery requests and in a deposition.

The court reasoned that the improper conduct impeded the administration of justice, unduly complicated the proceedings, and caused the court to make false factual findings. The court ordered the person engaging in the misdeeds to pay 100% of the fees incurred in connection with the motion for sanctions and 33% of the fees incurred in litigating the merits of the case, which resulted in an award of over $7 million in fees and expenses.

In upholding that civil penalty, the Delaware Supreme Court described the errant conduct in detail. For example, a Party's cell phone with relevant data was allegedly "dropped in a plastic cup of Diet Coke." Although the company involved in the stockholder dispute was in the business of providing forensic services to preserve and retrieve electronic data, the party involved merely asked an assistant with no expertise in forensics, to attempt to dry-out the phone. After that meager effort was unsuccessful, instead of having an expert attempt to retrieve the data from the phone, the phone was discarded. The Court of Chancery found that explanation unbelievable and so did the Supreme Court.

In addition, the party penalized had deleted approximately 20,000 emails the day before making an image of data on his laptop. He also emptied the recycle bin on his laptop that was used to delete the emails. Notably, his recycle bin was not emptied on a regular basis prior to this deletion. Browser history and files created by application software were also deleted. Subsequent forensic examination revealed that shadow copies were routinely created by the operating system, unbeknownst to the person who deleted the emails. As a result, the vast majority of them were recovered.

The court found that the intentional destruction of information after the court had entered an order requiring the production of that information, and recklessly failing to safeguard evidence on the cell phone which was regularly used to exchange text messages, made an important source of discovery unavailable. Together with repeatedly lying to conceal aspects of the deletion of information, these actions constituted bad faith.

Importantly, there is no requirement that a person who deletes discoverable information succeed in his efforts to thwart the ability of an opposing party to prosecute the merits of the case. Penalties can be imposed for bad faith tactics even if those tactics are not successful in thwarting litigation, or delaying it, or making it unnecessarily complicated.

This decision on penalties is useful as a reference tool for litigators who seek to incentivize both their clients and opposing parties to play by the rules, especially if they hope to avoid expensive penalties for noncompliance. *See Shawe v. Elting*, Del. Supr., No. 487, 2016 (Feb. 13, 2017). ◆

Francis G.X. Pileggi, Esquire, is the member-in-charge of the Wilmington, Delaware, office of Eckert Seamans Cherin & Mellott, LLC. He summarizes key corporate and commercial decisions of Delaware Courts, and addresses legal ethics, at www.delawarelitigation.com.

Delaware Disbars Pennsylvania Lawyer

The Delaware Supreme Court in a recent decision disbarred an out-of-state lawyer who had been admitted pro hac vice in Delaware litigation. When applied to an attorney not admitted in the state, Delaware's high court explained that disbarment means the unconditional exclusion from the admission to, or the exercise of any privilege to, practice law in the state.

This recent decision involved a Pennsylvania lawyer who was admitted pro hac vice to represent a Delaware doctor in a Delaware medical malpractice action. The disbarment stemmed from the lawyer's intentional misconduct that included the failure to disclose altered medical records and the failure to correct his client's false testimony.

The Delaware Supreme Court adopted the findings of the Board on Professional Responsibility, which concluded that the lawyer's actions were "at best dishonest and at worst criminal [and] resulted in actual and potential harm to the litigants, the judicial process and the public."

The specific Delaware Rules of Professional Conduct that were violated included Rules 3.3(b); 3.4(a); 3.4 (c); 4.1(b); 8.4(c); and 8.4(d)—based on the following findings: (1) failure to take reasonable remedial measures by failing to disclose to the tribunal the criminal and/or fraudulent conduct of the client; (2) unlawfully concealing a material document having potential evidentiary value; (3) failing to disclose a material fact when disclosure was necessary to avoid assisting a fraudulent act by a client; (4) engaging in conduct involving dishonesty, fraud, deceit or misrepresentation by failing to provide the relevant documents to the opposing party or the tribunal; and (5) by engaging in conduct that was prejudicial to the administration of justice by failing to disclose material documents.

The specific factual background involved the alteration of medical records by a medical doctor regarding the condition of the patient. This was a central issue in the medical malpractice case against the medical doctor. The medical doctor and her staff changed the treatment notes to alter the description of the actual condition of the patient, as well as what follow-up advice the medical doctor had given to the patient.

It was not until a subsequent lawsuit against the attorney representing the medical doctor for bad faith and legal malpractice took place, that both the existence of the altered medical records and the failure to produce them during the medical negligence litigation was first uncovered.

The altered medical records were of significant evidentiary value and had a substantial impact on the amount of the jury verdict. The medical doctor testified at her deposition that the office records produced in her discovery were complete, even though they did not include the altered records that she had reviewed with her counsel. The medical doctor also testified, both in her deposition and at trial, that she had not reviewed anything other than the documents that had been produced.

The disbarred attorney did not correct the false deposition testimony, nor did he correct the false trial testimony. It was also a violation of the Rules of Professional Conduct for the disbarred attorney not to supplement discovery responses—by failing to disclose the altered medical records. It was also a failure of his ethical obligation not to notify the opposing counsel and the court about the fraudulent actions and the false testimony of his client.

The rule involved in this case with the most widespread applicability to general litigation is Rule 3.3(b), which subjects lawyers to penalties if they fail to take reasonable remedial measures by failing to disclose to the tribunal, any litigation-related criminal and/or fraudulent conduct of a client. In this case, that rule was violated based on the awareness of the attorney of medical records that were altered by his client, and allowing his client to testify falsely during her deposition and at trial without disclosing that fraud and falsity. Moreover, and similarly, Rule 3.4(a) makes it unlawful to conceal a material document having potential evidentiary value by failing to disclose the existence of such a document. In this context, concealment is defined as failing to disclose.

Although less likely to be encountered by most lawyers, also important is the requirement that a lawyer disclose a material fact when disclosure is necessary to avoid assisting a fraudulent act by a client. As applied to this case, the attorney violated Rule 4.1(b) by failing to disclose the existence of altered medical records, which was a material fact in the medical malpractice action where the care provided was the central issue in the case. Failing to disclose the existence of the material medical records with obvious evidentiary value was also a violation of Rule 8.4(d), which provides that it is professional misconduct for a lawyer to engage in conduct that is prejudicial to the administration of justice. Failure of a lawyer to disclose documentation that he knows to be of material evidentiary value is prejudicial to the administration of justice.

Disbarment is an appropriate penalty generally when a lawyer engages in intentional misconduct involving dishonesty, fraud, deceit or misrepresentation that seriously and adversely reflect on the ability of the lawyer's fitness to practice. There are 11 aggravating factors and 13 mitigating factors that the court considers in connection with its analysis of this issue, none of which helped the attorney involved avoid disbarment.

In closing, the court cited two decisions in other jurisdictions that found disbarment to be appropriate when lawyers intentionally concealed evidence and assisted their clients with testifying falsely. The conclusion reached in this case was also supported by the grave violations of the standards of conduct that must be upheld in the legal profession. ◆

Francis G.X. Pileggi, Esquire is the member-in-charge of the Wilmington, Delaware, office of Eckert Seamans Cherin & Mellott, LLC. He summarizes key corporate and commercial decisions of Delaware Courts, and addresses legal ethics, at www.delawarelitigation.com.